*R*OADS TO RIDE
SOUTH

HEYDAY BOOKS

ROADS TO RIDE

SOUTH

A Bicyclist's
Topographic Guide
to San Mateo,
Santa Clara, and
Santa Cruz Counties

By
Grant Petersen
and
John Kluge

This book is dedicated
to Jim Johnston and Mike
Zickerman.

Cover photo: Lobitos Creek Rd.
in San Mateo County by
Doug Matsumoto.

Photos opposite pages 1, 24,
52, 67, 98, 99, 112, and on 130 by
Doug Matsumoto. All other
photos by Grant Petersen.

Editor and Production
Manager: Tom Schmitz

Design: Dennis Gallagher

Production: Alicia Hart, Jean
McLaughlin, Nancy Webb

Cartography: Sarah Levin

Proofreading: Rina Margolin

Copyright © 1985 by
Grant Petersen and John Kluge

Printed in the United States of
America.

10 9 8 7 6 5 4 3 2

Published by
Heyday Books
Box 9145
Berkeley, California 94709

ISBN: 0-930588-17-7
Library of Congress Catalog
Card: 84-82439

Acknowledgments

Several people helped with this book in various capacities. In no particular order, they are:

Mary Anderson, for organizing, driving, encouragement

Ken Bechtol, for driving

Doug Matsumoto, for driving and photographing

Rich Davies, for lending his altimeter

Bob Leibold and Velo Promo, for advice and knowledge. (The best deal around is Velo Promo's cycling map of Santa Cruz County. It's a beautiful, informative map, and is available through Velo Promo, 414½ Soquel Drive, Santa Cruz, 95062. It costs only $1.00.)

Bob Ward, for proofreading the text, and advice

Tony Ward, for the same

The staff at Palo Alto Bike Shop, for helpful suggestions

Tom Ritchey, for lots of things to think about

Beth Linder, for driving and riding

Gary McCurdy, for riding

The staff at Heyday Books, for their help

Lisa B. Porter, for driving

Mark Krizack, for his knowledge of wheelchairs and riders

Judy Benoit, for her time and knowledge

Gary Kerr, for his time and knowledge

Peter Rich, for advice

Ramona d'Viola, for her time and modelling (that's her on the cover)

many other friends and family, for general support

Olga Petersen, for her generosity.

Alpine Rd.

Contents

A sample road is diagrammed here to describe the notations used in this book.

Sample Rd.

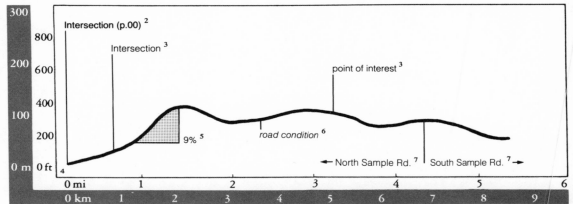

1. The county in which the road appears is indicated. San Mateo roads can be found on the county map on page 3; Santa Clara roads on page 35; Santa Cruz roads on pages 82 and 83.

2. Intersecting roads that are profiled elsewhere in the book are printed in bold letters. Page numbers indicate where in the book the roads appear.

3. Non-profiled roads and other landmarks or points of interest are printed in lighter letters.

4. "0 ft" is the lowest point on the road, and other elevations are relative to it. Elevations do not refer to feet above sea level.

5. Grades are given as percentages, not degrees. Thus 9% means that the road rises 9 feet for every 100 feet it travels.

6. Road conditions are printed in light italics.

7. When a road changes name, it is shown by a name plus an arrow, usually beneath the profile.

Introduction

In this book you will find topographical profiles and brief descriptions of most of the enjoyable and useful roads in San Mateo, Santa Clara, and Santa Cruz Counties. Like *Roads to Ride: A Bicyclist's Topographic Guide to Alameda, Contra Costa, and Marin Counties,* this is a book of roads, rather than of rides, and as such, makes a few simple demands of the user. Its modular approach will not lead you by the handlebars on circuits of *our* choosing, but will allow you to piece together any type of ride *you* want to do. It should be interesting and valuable to riders who are unfamiliar with these roads as well as to

riders who already know them quite well. It's fun to look at objective comparisons of your favorite (or least favorite) hills.

The information was obtained by a method that has consistently proven its accuracy and reliability—we've ridden these roads by bicycle with particular attention to the immediate surroundings, and we drove them in a car, recording the objective data with a Thommen #2000 altimeter and an odometer. You can trust the information to be sufficiently complete and accurate to let you pick out the ride you want to do with the confidence that you won't be unpleasantly surprised. The text is

sparse by design, and any gaps will be filled in during your ride . . . as they should be. *How to use this book:* The book is divided into three sections— San Mateo County (pp. 1-31), Santa Clara County (pp. 33-79), and Santa Cruz County (pp. 81-127). At the beginning of each section are overall maps; the profiles are of individual roads in alphabetical order. To use this book, first plot out a trip on one of the overall maps, then look up the individual road profiles for details on topography and conditions. (If you have trouble finding a particular road, refer to the index at the back of the book). By working back and forth between the overall maps and the individual profiles, you'll be able to devise a trip closely suited to your needs.

Note to wheelchair athletes: We recognize that there is a large and growing number of athletes who cannot ride conventional bicycles and who get around in increasingly light, maneuverable, well-designed wheelchairs. (An experienced and fit wheelchair athlete can sometimes descend a hill faster than many bicyclists.) The information in this book should be of value to you as well. A short, beautiful, and relatively flat road such as Las Animas Rd. in eastern Santa Clara County may prove to be an ideal ride for beginning wheelchair athletes; those with more proven abilities might look for longer, more strenuous rides.

We hope you will like this book, and we welcome your comments.

Tunitas Creek Rd.

San Mateo County

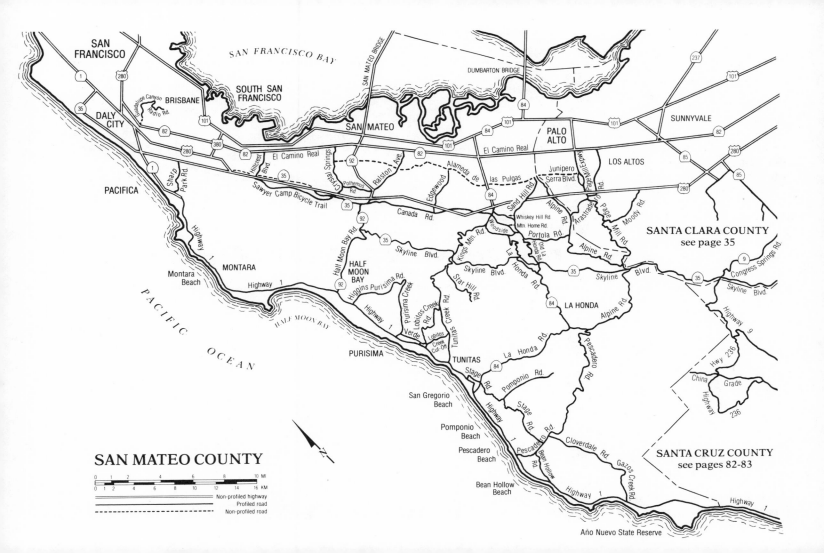

SAN FRANCISCO

SAN FRANCISCO BAY

BRISBANE

SOUTH SAN FRANCISCO

DALY CITY

PACIFICA

MONTARA

Montara Beach

PACIFIC OCEAN

HALF MOON BAY

PURISIMA

San Gregorio Beach

Pomponio Beach

Pescadero Beach

Bean Hollow Beach

SAN MATEO

SAN MATEO BRIDGE

DUMBARTON BRIDGE

PALO ALTO

SUNNYVALE

El Camino Real

LOS ALTOS

SANTA CLARA COUNTY
see page 35

El Camino Real

Alameda de las Pulgas

Edgewood

Canada Rd.

Junipero Serra Blvd.

Sand Hill Rd.

Whiskey Hill Rd.
Mtn. Home Rd.

Woodside

Portola Rd.

Alpine Rd.

Arastradero Rd.

Page Mill Rd.

Moody Rd.

Kings Mtn. Rd.

Skyline Blvd.

La Honda Rd.

Old La Honda Rd.

Alpine Rd.

Skyline Blvd.

Skyline Blvd.

Congress Springs Rd.

Skyline Blvd.

LA HONDA

Alpine Rd.

Pescadero Rd.

Highway 9

Hwy 236

China Grade

Highway 236

Hillcrest Blvd.

Crystal Springs

El Camino Real

Polhemus Rd.

Ralston Ave.

Sawyer Camp Bicycle Trail

Half Moon Bay Rd.

Skyline Blvd.

HALF MOON BAY

Higgins Purisima Rd.

Purisima Creek

Lobitos Creek Rd.

Star Hill Rd.

Verde

Lobitos Creek Cut-Off

Tunitas Creek Rd.

TUNITAS

Stage Rd.

La Honda Rd.

Pomponio Rd.

Stage Rd.

Pescadero Rd.

Cloverdale Rd.

Bean Hollow Rd.

Gazos Creek Rd.

SANTA CRUZ COUNTY
see pages 82-83

Highway 1

Highway 1

Highway 1

Sharp Park Rd.

Guadalupe Canyon Radio Rd.

N

SAN MATEO COUNTY

0 1 2   4   6   8   10 MI
0 1 2   4   6   8 10 12 14 16 KM

——— Non-profiled highway
━━━ Profiled road
- - - Non-profiled road

Año Nuevo State Reserve

Alpine Rd.

The northern end of Alpine Rd. is at the edge of the Stanford University campus, where it is a wide and developed but not congested urban road. West of Portola Rd. it narrows, becoming less developed and carrying less traffic. As it climbs, it follows Corte Madera Creek along a shaded hillside, and has a rough surface. When you reach the gate, stay to the right; the next 2½ miles are on a narrow, rutted dirt road bordered by oaks and chapparal. Balloon

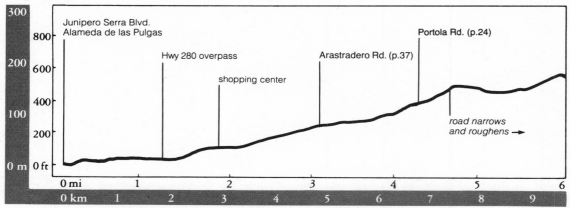

Alpine Rd. *cont.*

tires will be appreciated here, but standard tires and a little careful maneuvering will serve you just fine. This section is off limits to motor vehicles, and is a lot of fun. When the pavement resumes just past a second gate, the road becomes Page Mill Rd. until it reaches Skyline Blvd., about 2/3 of a mile. West of Skyline, Alpine Rd. winds through a stand of oaks, then descends into open pastures, passing through a dense oak-madrone forest shortly after it meets Por-

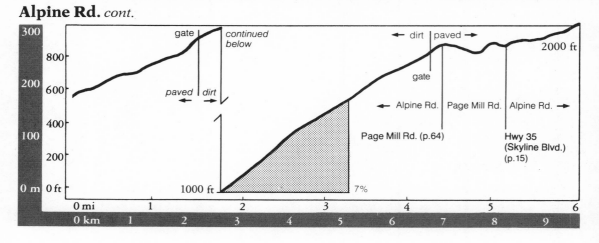

Alpine Rd. *cont.*

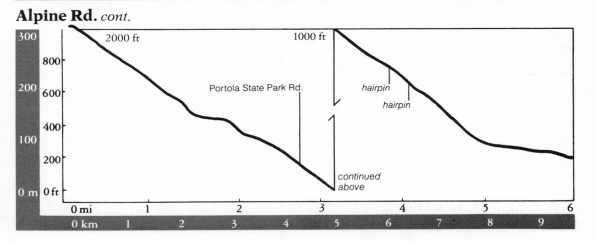

2000 ft

1000 ft

Portola State Park Rd.

hairpin

hairpin

continued
above

0 mi   1   2   3   4   5   6

0 km   1   2   3   4   5   6   7   8   9

tola State Park Rd. The road
then follows a creek through a
beautiful stand of redwoods.
The surface here is particularly
narrow and rough, with many
turns which demand your full
attention. This section of Alpine
Rd. is best for riding in the cooler months and on weekdays,
when traffic is lightest.

Alpine Rd. *cont.*

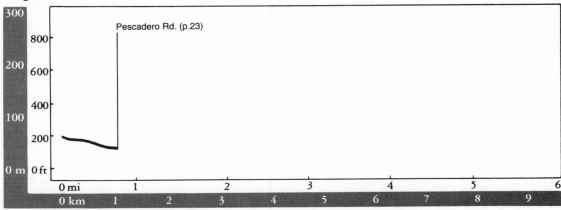

Pescadero Rd. (p.23)

0 mi   1   2   3   4   5   6

0 km   1   2   3   4   5   6   7   8   9

Bean Hollow Rd.

A narrow road with a rather rough surface. It travels over rolling coastal farmland between Pescadero Rd. and Hwy 1, passing a few farm houses and an artichoke farm. There's a nice view of the coast from the upper stretch, and almost no car traffic.

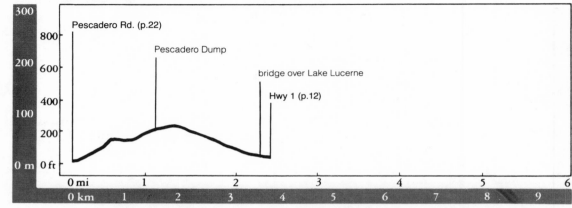

Canada Rd.

A very popular road, Canada (pronounced "Kenyatta") more or less parallels Hwy 280 along gentle hills overlooking Upper Crystal Springs Reservoir. It is very straight and fairly level (rare in San Mateo County) with a good surface and an ample shoulder, making for enjoyable, easy riding. Canada has the added advantage of being closed to motor vehicles on the first and third Sundays of the month, April through October. At other times it carries a steady

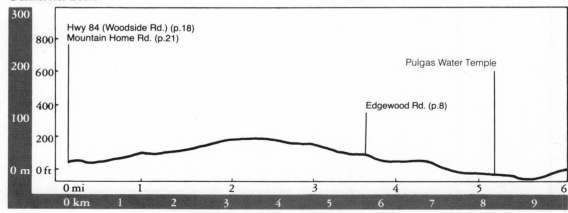

Canada Rd. *cont.*

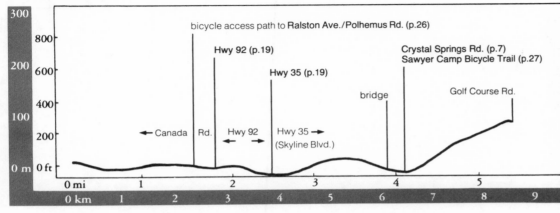

but well-behaved flow of traffic. This profile also includes the somewhat confusing upper portion of Skyline above Hwy 92, which allows for continued riding along Lower Crystal Springs Reservoir, and access to the Sawyer Camp Bicycle Trail.

Crystal Springs Rd.

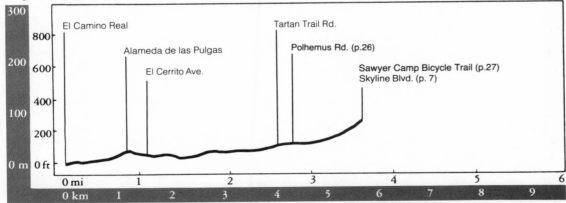

The eastern portion, between El Camino Real and El Cerrito Ave., is a fairly busy residential road. Beyond that it is a rural two-lane road lined with oaks, buckeyes, pines, and eucalyptus.

Edgewood Rd.

This is a well-travelled road that runs up the eastern slope of the coastal hills just south of San Carlos, and just west of Redwood City. It hasn't any interesting or prominent features, isn't particularly scenic, and is best regarded as a way into and out of the Crystal Springs area. It has bike lanes, and except for the very bottom, is undeveloped.

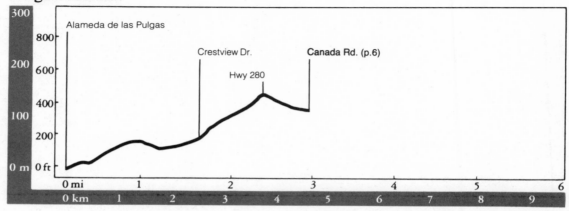

Gazos Creek Rd. / Cloverdale Rd.

Gazos Creek Rd. is a dirt and gravel logging road that travels inland from the coast, following Gazos Creek through brushy, dusty hillsides and farmland. After about two miles, Gazos Creek Rd. veers off sharply to Big Basin Redwoods State Park (this section is not profiled here) and Cloverdale Rd. begins. After a mile of easy climbing the road becomes paved, and travels through farm and pastureland in an open valley before joining up with Pescadero Rd.

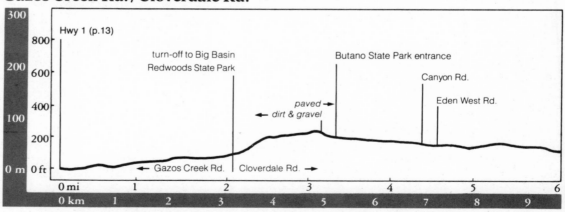

Alpine Rd.

Cloverdale Rd.

Gazos Creek Rd. / Cloverdale Rd. *cont.*

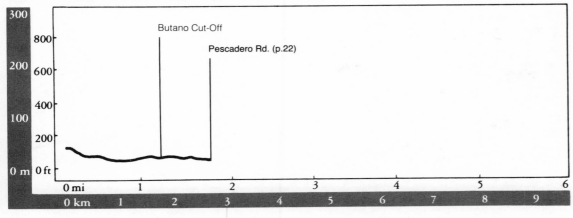

just east of the small town of Pescadero. The traffic is very light, and since these roads more or less parallel Hwy 1, they can be ridden as an alternative to it, making any long coastal ride more interesting.

Guadalupe Canyon Pkwy. / Radio Rd.

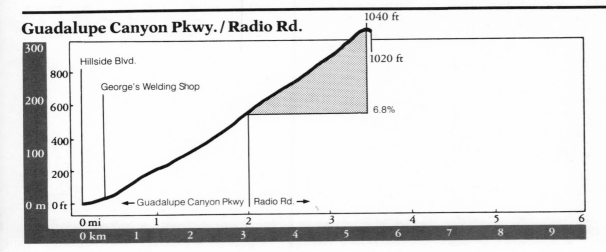

From Daly City, this is the way to the top of San Bruno Mtn. Guadalupe Canyon Pkwy. is quite wide and carries a fair amount of high-speed traffic. Radio Rd. is narrow with a rough surface, and after passing through a eucalyptus grove it winds its way to the radio tower at the summit. There's a good view, provided it's not foggy. Every New Year's Day there's a bicycle race to the top, beginning near George's Welding Shop on Guadalupe Canyon Pkwy.

In San Mateo County, Hwy 1 is hillier and more scenic than in Santa Cruz. It climbs bluffs and provides excellent views of the ocean, passing by numerous beaches, lots of farmland, and many coastal towns. Perhaps its nicest feature is that Hwy 1 intersects with several challenging roads that provide excellent inland diversions, thus giving you the opportunity to escape its high speed traffic (lots of trailers and motor homes) as well as avoid the more monotonous sections.

Highway 1

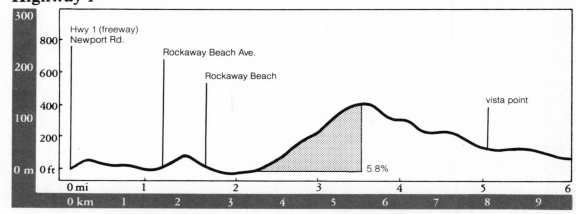

Highway 1 *cont.*

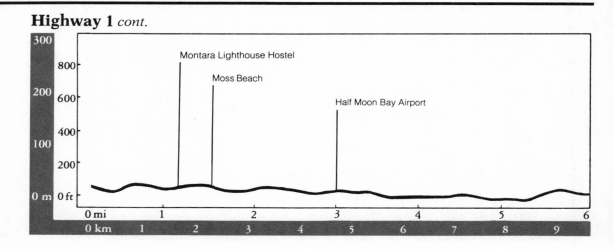

Highway 1 *cont.*

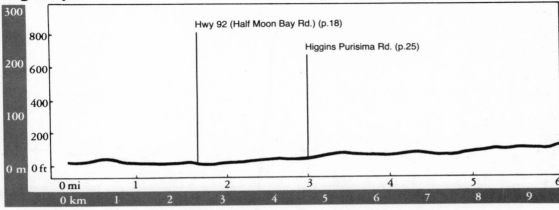

300
200
100
0 m

800
600
400
200
0 ft

Hwy 92 (Half Moon Bay Rd.) (p.18)

Higgins Purisima Rd. (p.25)

0 mi   1   2   3   4   5   6

0 km   1   2   3   4   5   6   7   8   9

Highway 1 *cont.*

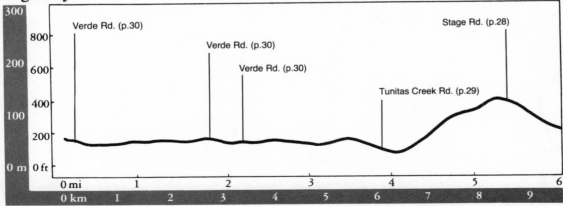

300
200
100
0 m

800
600
400
200
0 ft

Verde Rd. (p.30)

Verde Rd. (p.30)

Verde Rd. (p.30)

Stage Rd. (p.28)

Tunitas Creek Rd. (p.29)

0 mi   1   2   3   4   5   6

0 km   1   2   3   4   5   6   7   8   9

Highway 1 *cont.*

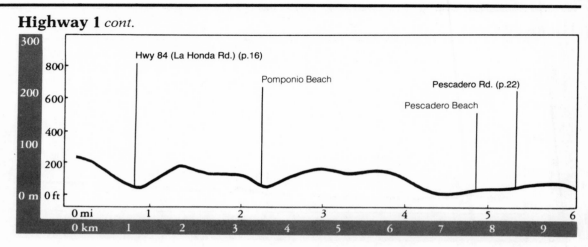

- Hwy 84 (La Honda Rd.) (p.16)
- Pomponio Beach
- Pescadero Rd. (p.22)
- Pescadero Beach

Highway 1 *cont.*

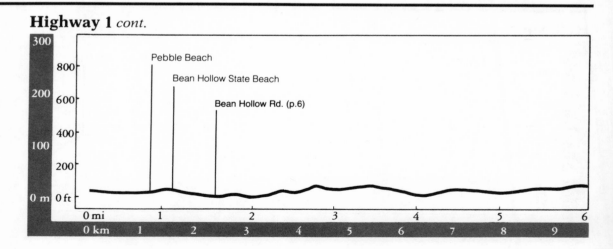

- Pebble Beach
- Bean Hollow State Beach
- Bean Hollow Rd. (p.6)

Highway 1 *cont.*

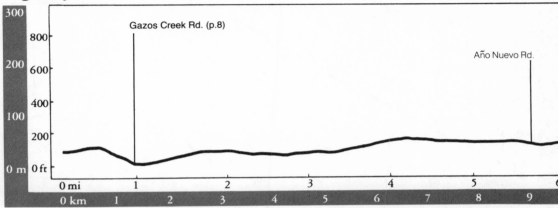

Gazos Creek Rd. (p.8)

Año Nuevo Rd.

300
800
200
600
400
100
200
0 m   0 ft

0 mi   1   2   3   4   5   6
0 km   1   2   3   4   5   6   7   8   9

Highway 1 *cont.*

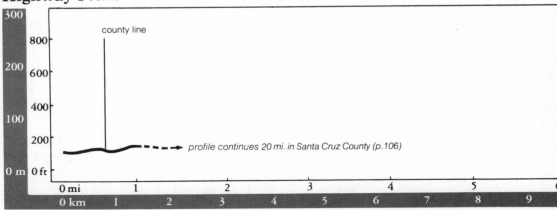

county line

profile continues 20 mi. in Santa Cruz County (p.106)

300
800
200
600
400
100
200
0 m   0 ft

0 mi   1   2   3   4   5   6
0 km   1   2   3   4   5   6   7   8   9

Highway 35 (Skyline Blvd.)

As the name implies, this road travels along a high ridge, providing distant views to both the east and west. As with most well-travelled roads, the county sees to it that the surface is well maintained, and that there's a decent shoulder. It runs a fairly direct north-south course, in and out of oak and redwood groves. This northern portion is noticeably cooler than the Santa Cruz County section, and it's common to be riding through thick clouds of fog even

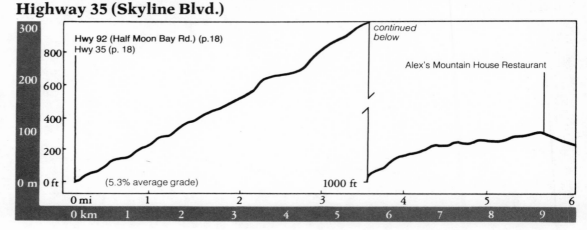

Hwy 92 (Half Moon Bay Rd.) (p.18)
Hwy 35 (p. 18)

continued below

Alex's Mountain House Restaurant

(5.3% average grade)

1000 ft

Highway 35 *cont.*

during the summer months. Be prepared, and wear colorful clothing. (Note: a portion of Hwy 35 north of its junction with Hwy 92 can be found on the Hwy 92 profile, p.18, and on the Canada Rd. profile, p.7)

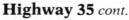

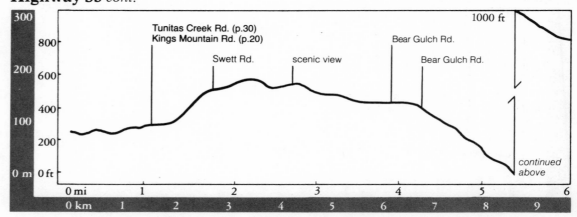

Tunitas Creek Rd. (p.30)
Kings Mountain Rd. (p.20)

Swett Rd.

scenic view

Bear Gulch Rd.

Bear Gulch Rd.

1000 ft

continued above

Highway 35 *cont.*

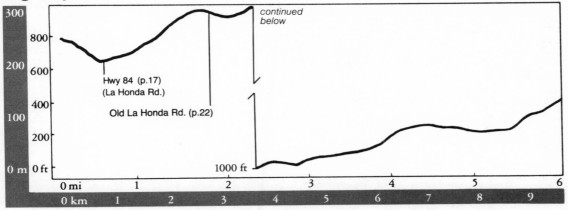

300
800
200
600
400
100
200
0 m 0 ft

Hwy 84 (p.17)
(La Honda Rd.)

Old La Honda Rd. (p.22)

continued below

1000 ft

0 mi   1   2   3   4   5   6
0 km   1   2   3   4   5   6   7   8   9

Highway 35 *cont.*

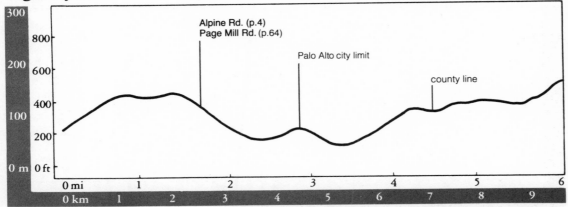

300
800
200
600
400
100
200
0 m 0 ft

Alpine Rd. (p.4)
Page Mill Rd. (p.64)

Palo Alto city limit

county line

0 mi   1   2   3   4   5   6
0 km   1   2   3   4   5   6   7   8   9

Highway 35 *cont.*

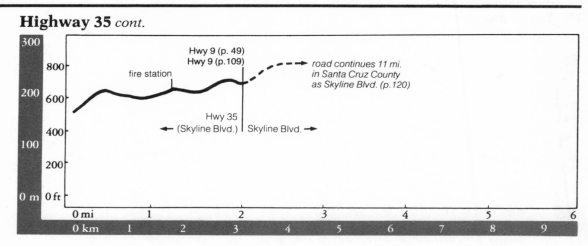

Highway 84 (La Honda Rd.)

As a main road between the coast and Woodside, La Honda Rd. is popular among both bicyclists and car people. It winds up a wooded canyon alongside San Gregorio and La Honda Creeks, gradually climbing to its highest elevation at Skyline Blvd. Between this point and the town of Woodside, it travels through a dense forest, and has many sharp turns.

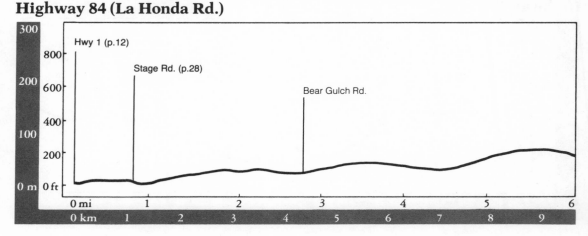

Highway 84 *cont.*

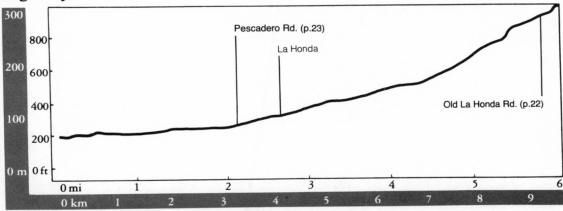

Pescadero Rd. (p.23)

La Honda

Old La Honda Rd. (p.22)

Highway 84 *cont.*

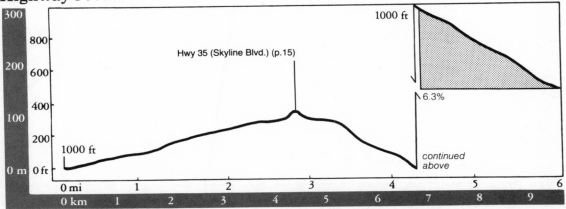

Hwy 35 (Skyline Blvd.) (p.15)

1000 ft

6.3%

1000 ft

continued above

Highway 84 *cont.*

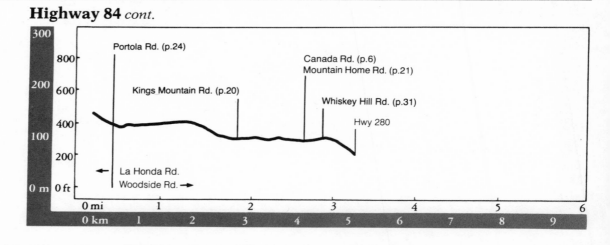

Portola Rd. (p.24)

Kings Mountain Rd. (p.20)

Canada Rd. (p.6)
Mountain Home Rd. (p.21)

Whiskey Hill Rd. (p.31)

Hwy 280

← La Honda Rd.
Woodside Rd. →

Highway 92 (Half Moon Bay Rd.)

Half Moon Bay Road runs between the coast and the northern part of Skyline Blvd. Though it passes through nice, brushy coastal hills and farmland, there seems to be a constant stream of traffic on it, completely spoiling it for bicyclists. During weekends and at rush hour, it is often bumper-to-bumper. For a nice ride between the coast and inland San Mateo County, Tunitas Creek Rd. (to the south) is a much better choice.

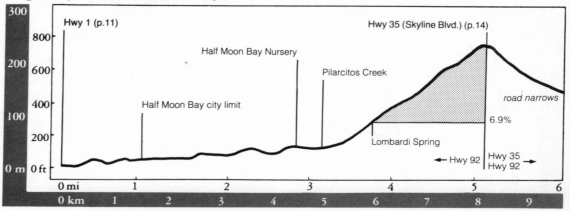

Hwy 1 (p.11)

Hwy 35 (Skyline Blvd.) (p.14)

Half Moon Bay Nursery

Pilarcitos Creek

road narrows

Half Moon Bay city limit

6.9%

Lombardi Spring

← Hwy 92

Hwy 35
Hwy 92

Highway 92 *cont.*

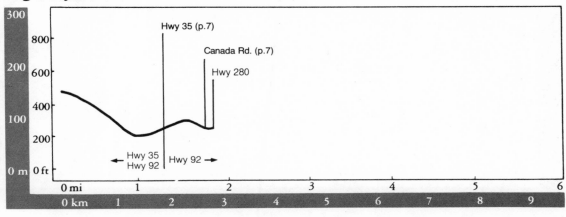

Hwy 35 (p.7)

Canada Rd. (p.7)

Hwy 280

← Hwy 35 Hwy 92   Hwy 92 →

Hillcrest Blvd.

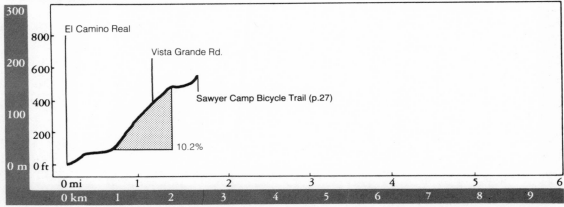

El Camino Real

Vista Grande Rd.

Sawyer Camp Bicycle Trail (p.27)

10.2%

This wide, smooth, purely residential road is quite steep, and is worth using only as an access route to better riding. Don't descend it without good brakes.

A strenuous climb and an exhilarating descent. The lower portion is lush, with a few houses. As it climbs, the surface quality worsens for a mile or so, then greatly improves as the road continues, hairpin after hairpin, up the steep, over-grown eastern slopes of Skyline Ridge. There can be a bother-some amount of motor traffic on weekends, but generally it isn't too bad, and it's a wider road than many of the other steep, winding roads in the area.

Kings Mountain Rd.

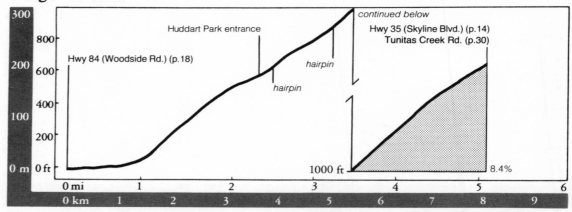

A narrow cut-off between Tuni-tas Creek Rd. and Verde Rd., it has a rough surface, almost no traffic, and travels over low and brushy coastal mounds.

Lobitos Creek Cut-Off

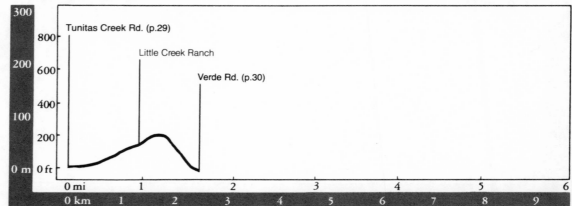

Lobitos Creek Rd.

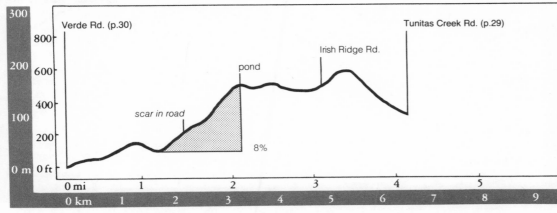

Verde Rd. (p.30)
Tunitas Creek Rd. (p.29)
Irish Ridge Rd.
pond
scar in road
8%

An unpaved, narrow road that rolls over poison oak covered hills and horse pastures, Lobitos Creek Rd. is particularly beautiful and enjoyable when the hills are green and the road is dry. Even with 1¼″ tires you'll have to do a small amount of navigating to get past some of the loose dirt and ruts in the road, so if you have a ballooner, use it here. Essentially no traffic.

Mountain Home Rd.

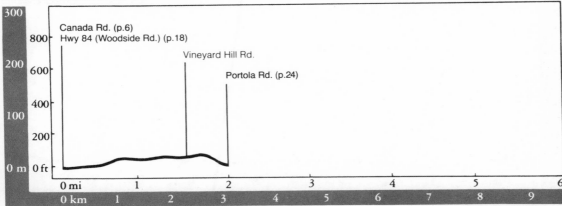

Canada Rd. (p.6)
Hwy 84 (Woodside Rd.) (p.18)
Vineyard Hill Rd.
Portola Rd. (p.24)

A shoulderless residential road between Woodside Rd. and Portola Rd. It is crowded by eucalyptus, oaks, ivy, and assorted shrubs, and is almost entirely in the shade. There are many gentle curves on a washboard surface, and moderate local traffic.

This begins as a narrow, steep residential road with many tight turns. You can climb it at full effort, but descending it safely requires constant braking. The traffic is bearable during midday, but in the mornings and evenings it gets quite bothersome. Southwest of Skyline Blvd. the road is unpaved and a lot less developed, with very little traffic. It travels along a forested hillside and is a lot of fun in dry conditions—particularly on a ballooner.

Old La Honda Rd.

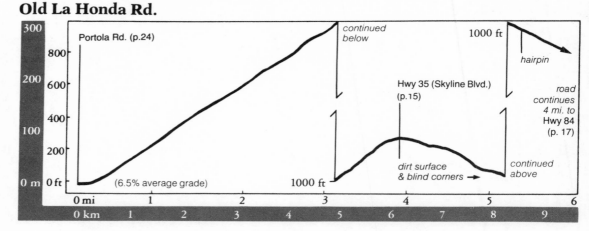

This is a beautiful, narrow, lightly travelled road. Starting from its western end right at the coast, it travels over open farmland and marshes, then climbs into a thick redwood forest, eventually meeting up with La Honda Rd. on the northern side of Sam McDonald Park. Along the way, it passes through the small settlements of Pescadero and Loma Mar, but these are easily missed, and you won't have to slow down significantly as you pass through them.

Pescadero Rd.

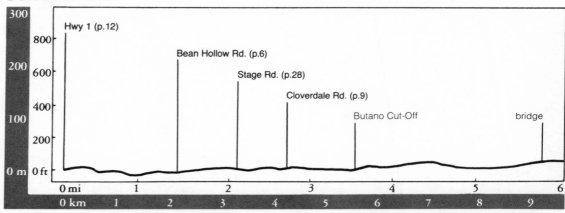

Pescadero Rd. *cont.*

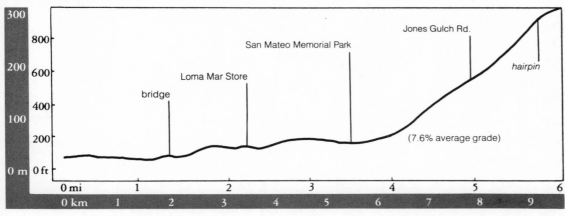

300 | **800** | **200** | **600** | **100** | **400** | **200** | **0 m** | **0 ft**

Jones Gulch Rd.

San Mateo Memorial Park

hairpin

Loma Mar Store

bridge

(7.6% average grade)

0 mi 1 2 3 4 5 6

0 km 1 2 3 4 5 6 7 8 9

Pescadero Rd. *cont.*

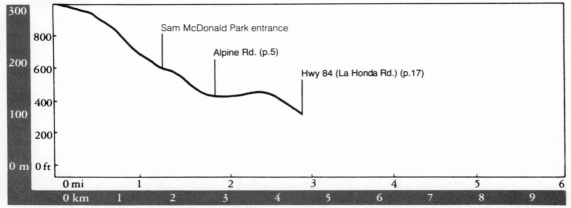

300 | **800** | **200** | **600** | **100** | **400** | **200** | **0 m** | **0 ft**

Sam McDonald Park entrance

Alpine Rd. (p.5)

Hwy 84 (La Honda Rd.) (p.17)

0 mi 1 2 3 4 5 6

0 km 1 2 3 4 5 6 7 8 9

Pomponio Rd.

This is probably one of the least ridden roads in the South Bay. It's an all dirt road that heads east from Stage Rd., passes by farmland (flowers in the summer) and ends at a gate. Beyond this point, it's private. The surface is hard when dry, and smooth enough for standard tires and fast riding.

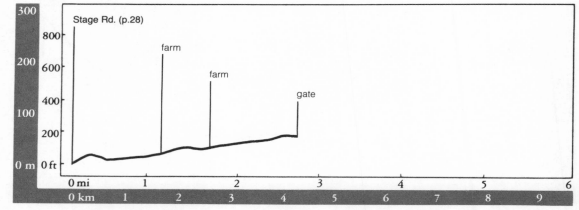

Portola Rd.

A wooded urban road in Portola Valley. It's kind of a pretty road, but too heavily used by cars to be really excellent for bicycles. It has bike lanes.

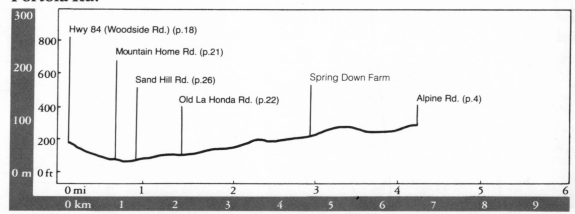

Pomponio Rd.

Purisima Creek Rd.

Purisima Creek Rd. / Higgins Purisima Rd.

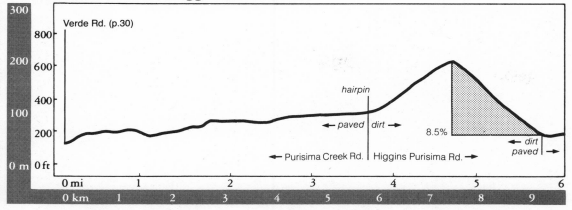

These two roads comprise a diversion from Hwy 1 just south of Half Moon Bay. Purisima Creek Rd. is narrow, with a rough, patched surface that rolls and bumps you along a small hillside above and parallel to Purisima Creek. There's a hairpin at its eastern end, at which point the road switches back westward as the unpaved Higgins Purisima Rd. The dirt surface is hard and rocky, but there are no large, unavoidable boulders or deep ruts, and it's

Purisima Creek Rd. / Higgins Purisima Rd. *cont.*

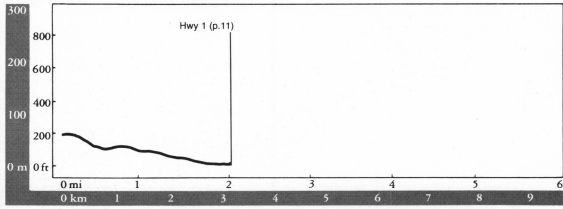

rideable even when wet. The northwestern section is paved and rural, also parallels the creek, and passes through farmland. Each spring, these roads are part of the Pinkie's Road Race course.

The eastern end of Ralston Ave. is four lanes wide, developed, residential, and busy. The climb begins in a half-in-the-gutter bike lane, which soon hops up onto the sidewalk and stays there most of the way to the top. Polhemus Road is a wide, smooth, unshaded road that travels through much less developed hillsides to Crystal Springs Road. (note: just west of the summit, there's a Cal-Trans Park & Ride facility, and a mile-long bicycle pathway to Canada Road)

Ralston Ave. / Polhemus Rd.

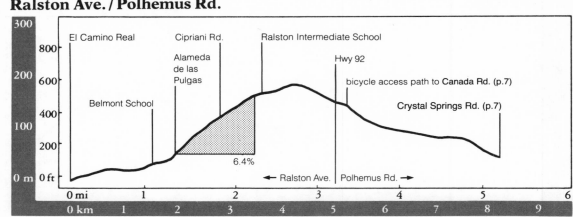

Between Alameda de las Pulgas and Hwy 280, this is a divided urban road with a smooth surface. It passes several new business developments, has plenty of car traffic, but is wide enough so that you won't feel crowded. West of 280, it's a two-lane rural road through relatively undeveloped hillsides.

Sand Hill Rd.

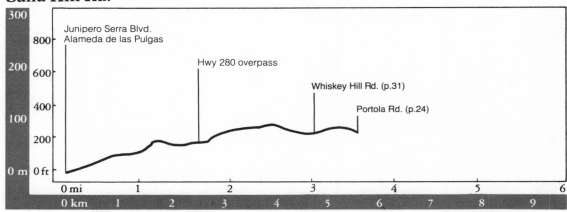

Sawyer Camp Bicycle Trail

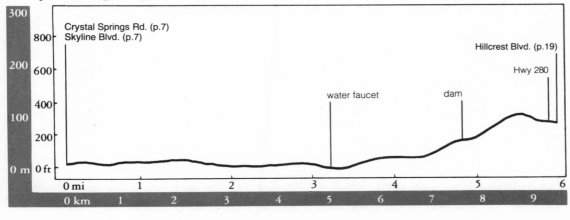

Crystal Springs Rd. (p.7)
Skyline Blvd. (p.7)

Hillcrest Blvd. (p.19)

Hwy 280

water faucet

dam

It's tempting, but misleading, to call this an ideal beginner's ride, because anybody can enjoy this car-less, flat, meandering trail as it travels through the densely forested hills above Crystal Springs Reservoir. It looks like a miniature road, with dotted white lines and all, but the traffic consists of runners, walkers, and skaters. You are encouraged to ride single file, and at a moderate pace. There are several small picnic areas, a water faucet, and a telephone along the way.

Sharp Park Rd.

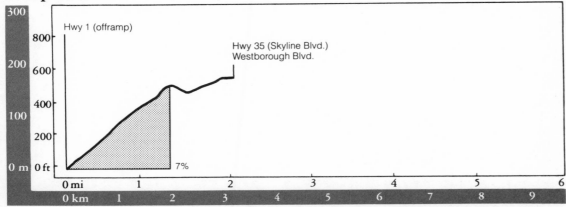

Hwy 1 (offramp)

Hwy 35 (Skyline Blvd.)
Westborough Blvd.

7%

This road's only value to a bicyclist is as a direct connector between Skyline and Hwy 1 in Pacifica—otherwise, it's not much fun. The uppermost end is wide, developed, and busy. The hill section is two lanes wide on the descent, one lane going up, with a lot of traffic and no shoulder. While it overlooks the ocean and some rolling farmland, the quick views you might get are not really worth the annoyance.

This is an excellent, interesting, and more strenuous alternative to Hwy 1 between Pescadero and San Gregorio. Except for the wider, better maintained couple of miles immediately north of Pescadero, it's a very narrow, rough-surfaced road which winds constantly through low coastal shrubs (heavy on the poison oak) and eucalyptus. There's a lot of eucalyptus debris on the road, and combined with any moisture at all, this makes for slip-

Stage Rd.

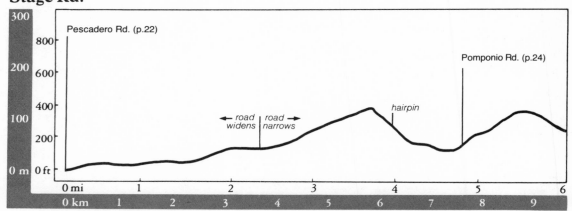

Pescadero Rd. (p.22)

Pomponio Rd. (p.24)

← road widens | road narrows →

hairpin

pery riding around the turns. There are good views of the surrounding hills, and almost no traffic.

Stage Rd. *cont.*

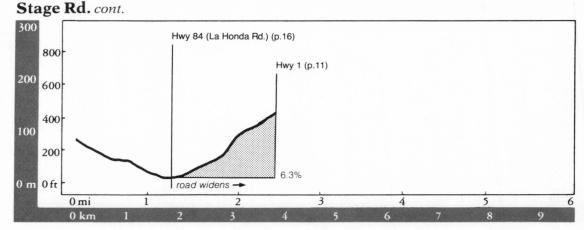

Hwy 84 (La Honda Rd.) (p.16)

Hwy 1 (p.11)

road widens →

6.3%

Star Hill Rd.

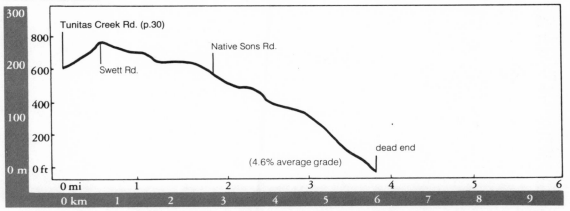

Tunitas Creek Rd. (p.30)

Swett Rd.

Native Sons Rd.

(4.6% average grade)

dead end

A very lightly travelled, un-paved, dead-end road that heads south from the summit of Tunitas Creek Rd. It winds gently along a steep hillside, thick with oaks and redwoods, and ends several hundred feet lower, overlooking an open meadow. The surface is generally hard and smooth. Any rim/tire combination that is presently on your bike should be sufficiently robust—many paved roads are a lot rougher.

Tunitas Creek Rd.

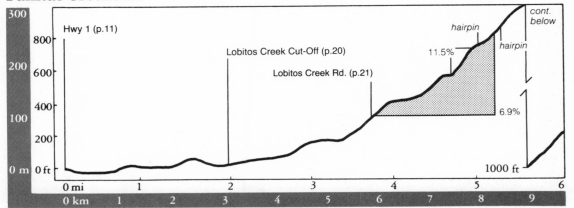

Hwy 1 (p.11)

Lobitos Creek Cut-Off (p.20)

Lobitos Creek Rd. (p.21)

hairpin

hairpin

11.5%

6.9%

1000 ft

cont. below

The most distinguishing feature of this narrow, curving road is its rough, patchwork surface. It appears as though the road crews are intent on repairing it, but never have enough tar and gravel to complete the job. Near the coast it travels over farmland, but for most of its length it parallels tiny, log-jammed Tunitas Creek through a lush forest of redwoods and scattered ferns. It is almost entirely in the shade, so it's a good hill to climb on a hot day. Descending

Tunitas Creek Rd. *cont.*

it safely demands your total attention and an untiring grip, and in the fall or early spring you can get chilled right to the bone. An excellent, challenging road, with very little traffic.

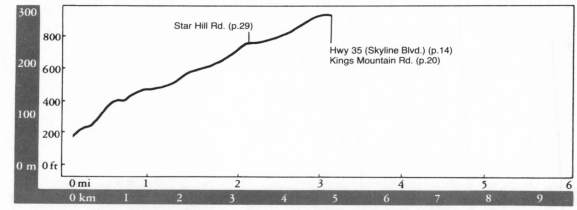

Verde Rd.

A narrow, rough-surfaced road that closely parallels Hwy 1 between the small towns of Lobitos and Purisima. It travels past coastal farms, provides good views to the west, and has almost no traffic. A peculiarity of this road is that it actually has three ends—all on Hwy 1.

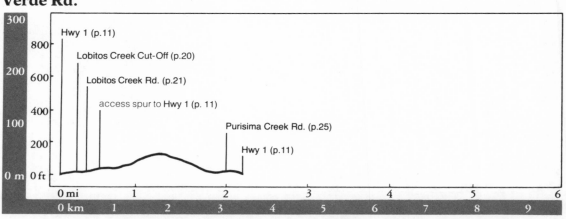

Whiskey Hill Rd.

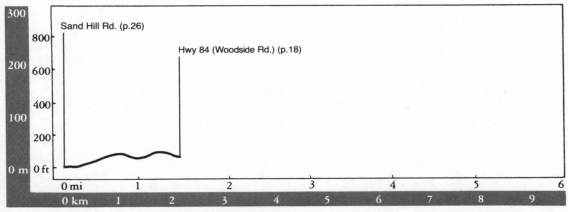

Sand Hill Rd. (p.26)

Hwy 84 (Woodside Rd.) (p.18)

A wide, smooth, urban road between Sand Hill Rd. and Woodside. The traffic isn't bad, and there are bike lanes.

West Quimby Rd.

Santa Clara County

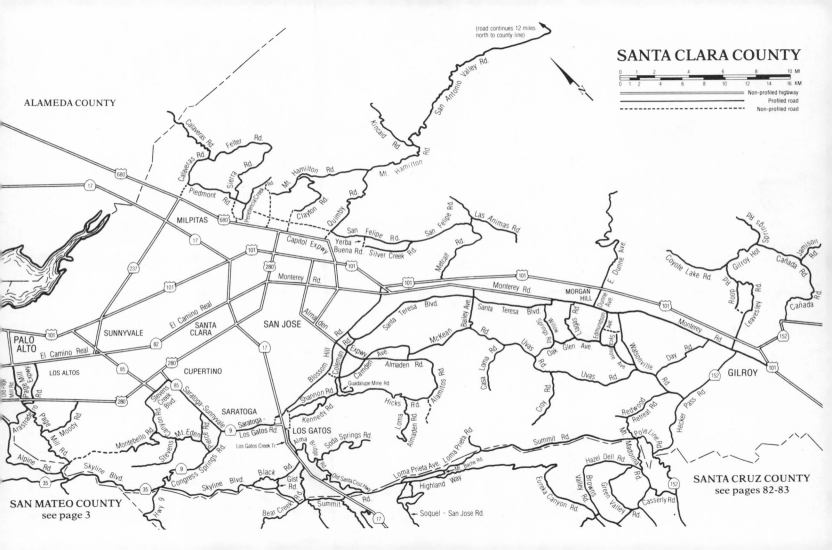

SANTA CLARA COUNTY

0 1 2 3 4 6 8 10 MI
0 2 4 6 8 10 12 14 16 KM

Non-profiled highway
Profiled road
Non-profiled road

N

(road continues 12 miles
north to county line)

ALAMEDA COUNTY

680

17

Calaveras Rd.
Felter Rd.
Sierra Rd.
Calaveras Rd.
Piedmont Rd.
Penitencia Creek Rd.

MILPITAS
680
17
237
101
280

Mt. Hamilton Rd.
Clayton Rd.
Quimby Rd.
Mt. Hamilton Rd.

San Antonio Valley Rd.
Kincaid Rd.

San Felipe Rd.
Las Animas Rd.
Metcalf
San Felipe Rd.

Capitol Expwy
Yerba Buena Rd.
Silver Creek Rd.

Monterey Rd.
101

Monterey Rd.
MORGAN HILL
101

Coyote Lake Rd.
Gilroy Hot Springs Rd.
Roop Rd.
Cañada Rd.
Jamison Rd.
Cañada Rd.
Leavesley Rd.

82
SUNNYVALE
SANTA CLARA
101
SAN JOSE

PALO ALTO
101
El Camino Real
El Camino Real
LOS ALTOS
85
280

Almaden Rd.
Santa Teresa Blvd.
Bailey Ave.
Santa Teresa Blvd.
Willow Springs Rd.
E. Dunne Ave.
Dunne Ave.
Edmundson Ave.

17
CUPERTINO
85
Saratoga-Sunnyvale Rd.
Stevens Creek Blvd.
SARATOGA

Blossom Hill Rd.
Coleman Expwy
Camden Ave.
Almaden Rd.
McKean Rd.
Casa Loma Rd.
Uvas Rd.
Oak Glen Ave.
Lopas Rd.
Watsonville Rd.
Day Rd.

Monterey Rd.
152
GILROY
152
101

Arastradero
Page Mill Rd.
Old Page Mill Rd.
Moody Rd.
Page Mill Rd.

280
Montebello Rd.
Stevens Canyon Rd.
Mt. Eden Rd.
9
Saratoga Los Gatos Rd.
Los Gatos Creek Tr.
LOS GATOS
Shannon Rd.
Kennedy Rd.
Guadalupe Mine Rd.
Hicks Rd.
Almaden Rd.
Alamitos Rd.
Loma Rd.
Croy Rd.
Uvas Rd.

Redwood Retreat Rd.
Pole Line Rd.
Mt. Madonna Rd.
Hecker Pass Rd.

Alpine Rd.
35
Skyline Blvd.
Hwy 9
Congress Springs Rd.
Skyline Blvd.
35
Black Rd.
Gist Rd.
Bear Creek Rd.
Summit
Alma Bridge Rd.
Soda Springs Rd.
Old Santa Cruz Hwy
Highland Way
Loma Prieta Ave.
Loma Prieta Rd.
Mt. Bache Rd.
Summit Rd.

Soquel - San Jose Rd.
17

Hazel Dell Rd.
Browns Valley Rd.
Green Valley Rd.
Eureka Canyon Rd.
Casserly Rd.

SANTA CRUZ COUNTY
see pages 82-83

SAN MATEO COUNTY
see page 3

Alma Bridge Rd.

This road travels above and closely parallel to the eastern shore of Lexington Reservoir, next to Hwy 17, south of Los Gatos. It is bordered on the east by tall hills covered with oaks, maples, poison oak, coyote bush, and a few redwoods and madrones. (If you'd like to get closer to these hills, ride up Soda Springs Rd.) Lexington Reservoir is a popular recreation area, and on fair-weather weekends the traffic can be steady, but it's never really thick.

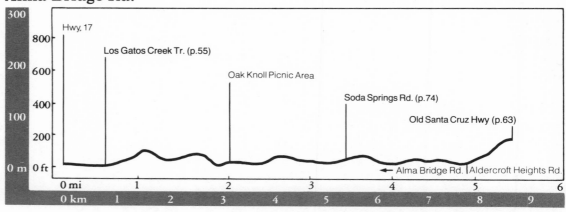

Almaden Expwy. / Almaden Rd.

Almaden Expwy. is four lanes wide, travels through a business district, carries a lot of traffic, and is not much fun. Almaden Rd. is a two lane rural road with less traffic, and is generally more enjoyable. As it gradually curves around to the west, it passes through New Almaden, changes names to Alamitos Rd., and eventually meets up with the south end of Hicks Rd.

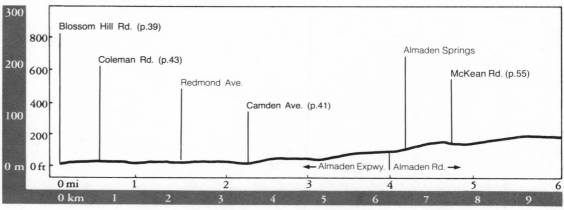

Almaden Expwy. / Almaden Rd. *(cont.)*

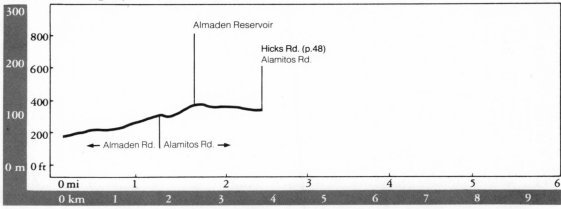

Arastradero Rd.

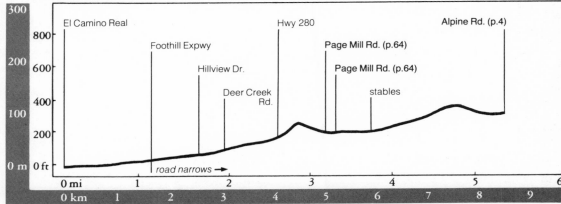

This road begins at El Camino Real as a four lane urban thoroughfare with bike lanes, narrowing to two lanes west of the Foothill Expwy. After a jog to the south at its intersection with Page Mill Rd., Arastradero carries less traffic and provides more enjoyable riding as it follows a creek along the border of a game refuge.

Bailey Ave.

The eastern portion of this road is four lanes wide and divided. As it heads west from Santa Teresa Blvd., it narrows quite a bit and climbs up to Calero Reservoir at McKean Rd. The surface is a bit rough, and the steep section is curvy.

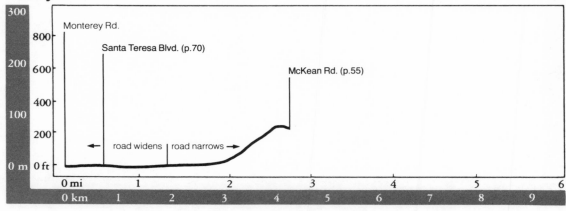

Black Rd.

This is an absolutely beautiful road that snakes through a dense oak and laurel forest between Hwy 17 and Skyline Blvd. It passes by a few homes and a school, but the traffic is light, and the riding is strenuous but excellent. Unfortunately, the intersection with Hwy 17 is effectively a dead end. Riding east, unless you have business down there, you would do well to loop back to Skyline Blvd. via Gist Rd—a short, steep and quite similar road.

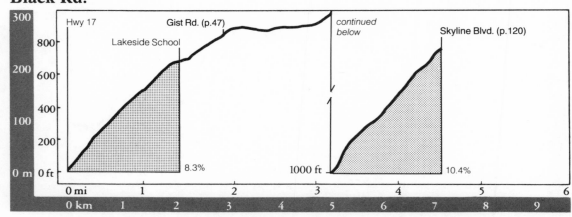

Blossom Hill Rd.

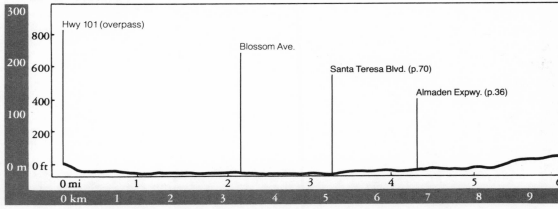

300
800
200
600
100
400
200
0 m   0 ft

Hwy 101 (overpass)

Blossom Ave.

Santa Teresa Blvd. (p.70)

Almaden Expwy. (p.36)

0 mi   1   2   3   4   5   6

0 km   1   2   3   4   5   6   7   8   9

In spite of its name, Blossom Hill Rd. is a heavily-developed, heavily-trafficked road that takes you on a tour of residences and shopping malls. "Main Street" would be a more fitting name. Ride it if you have to; there are bike lanes.

Blossom Hill Rd. *cont.*

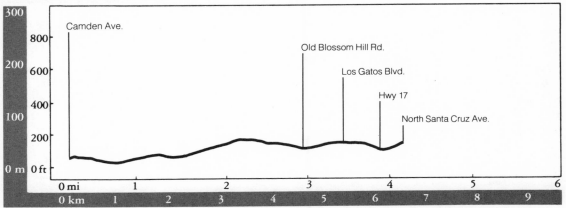

300
800
200
600
100
400
200
0 m   0 ft

Camden Ave.

Old Blossom Hill Rd.

Los Gatos Blvd.

Hwy 17

North Santa Cruz Ave.

0 mi   1   2   3   4   5   6

0 km   1   2   3   4   5   6   7   8   9

An excellent road. It winds
through oak-shaded hillsides
and open pastures on the western side of Calaveras Reservoir,
and provides you with the opportunity to work on your
climbing, descending, and cor-
nering skills. A narrow road
with a rough surface and light
traffic. Lots of fun.

Calaveras Rd.

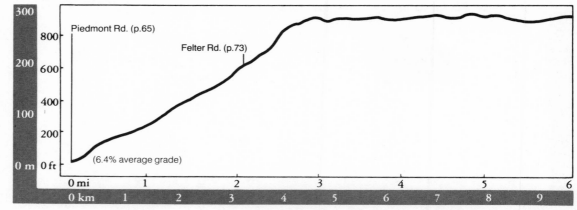

Piedmont Rd. (p.65)

Felter Rd. (p.73)

(6.4% average grade)

Calaveras Rd. *cont.*

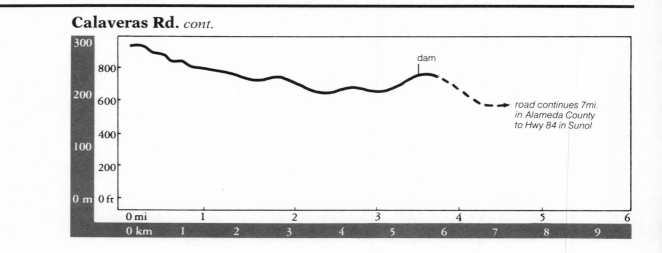

dam

road continues 7mi.
in Alameda County
to Hwy 84 in Sunol

Camden Ave.

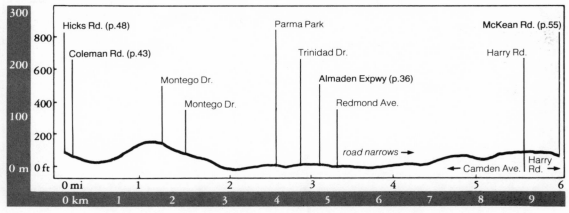

Between Hicks Rd. and Redmond Ave., this is a wide road past businesses and residences that carries a lot of traffic. East of Redmond Ave. it narrows, has less traffic, and is almost entirely residential. It has bike lanes, and connects many other useful roads in the area.

Cañada Rd.

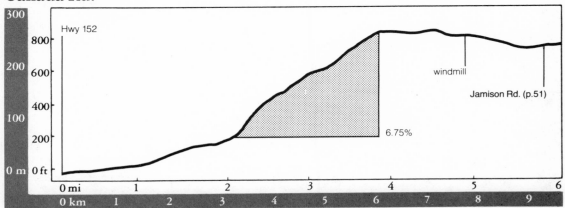

This may be my favorite road anywhere. The only wild turkeys I've ever seen ambled across the road about 60 feet in front of me one July afternoon. The lower southern portion follows a wooded creek and provides ample shade as you warm up for the climb ahead. As the road winds up the open pastures, you'll see staring cows, continuous fences, barns, windmills, and beautiful distant hills. The upper, rolling portion is the kind of road that you'll

wish would go on forever—
turns that you can accelerate
through, with several short,
easy hills that you can climb
without shifting out of your big
chainring. The northern portion is shaded by oaks, follows a
creek, and is home to at least
four turkeys; it ends at Gilroy
Hot Springs Rd. There's almost
no traffic.

Cañada Rd. *cont.*

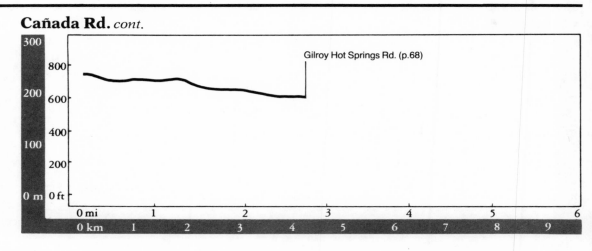

A short, narrow, rural road with
a rough surface. It follows Llagas Creek westward from the
junction of Uvas and McKean
Roads past residences and pastures. Not much traffic.

Casa Loma Rd.

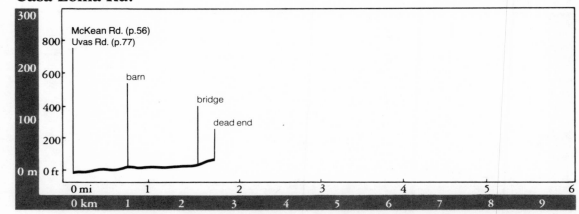

Clayton Rd.

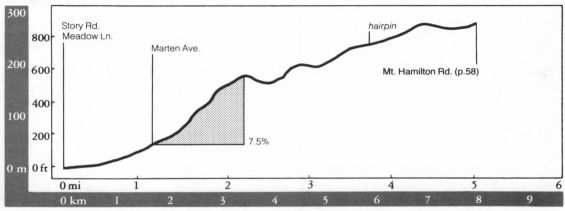

The lower portion of this road passes through tract housing before heading east, then north as it ascends some of the lower foothills of Mt. Hamilton. The bulk of the climb travels through rolling apricot orchards and past ranch houses. The descent is fast and fun. The surface is fine, and there isn't much traffic.

Coleman Rd./Guadalupe Mine Rd.

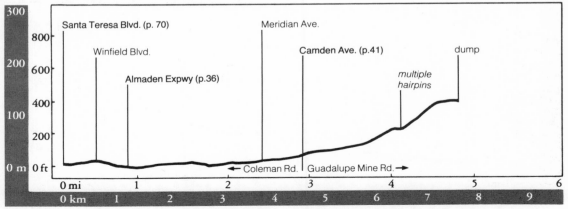

Coleman Rd. is a fairly wide, smooth road with a few houses along the way. It hasn't any particular aesthetic appeal, but it connects to other useful roads. Guadalupe Mine Rd., while it ends at a dump, does provide a challenging and interesting ride. It is heavily used during weekends, and isn't open later than 4:45 pm.

Coyote Lake Rd.

If you ride this once, you probably won't do so again. It's a narrow road that winds gently along a shaded hillside above Coyote Reservoir. However, the lake is also a favorite recreation spot for everyone within fifty miles who owns a boat and trailer, and the traffic is often stifling. If you're riding up Roop Rd. towards this road, I suggest you continue past it on Gilroy Hot Springs Rd., then circle back around on Cañada Rd.—a beautiful ride.

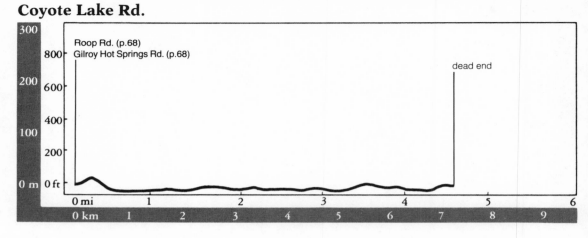

Croy Rd.

This road parallels Uvas Creek between Uvas Rd. and Uvas Canyon County Park. It travels over a series of small, rolling mounds, past a few ranches, and is partially shaded by redwoods and madrones. The road surface is quite a bit rougher beyond the bridge, and the last mile is very narrow. Campsites are available at the park at the end of the road. Traffic is light.

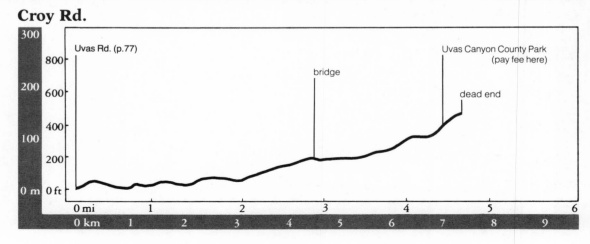

Day Rd.

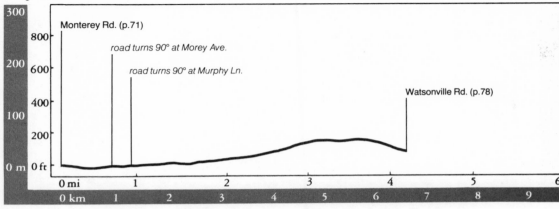

A plain, unexciting rural road over flat farmland and open pastures, just northwest of Gilroy. It has a decent surface, and light traffic.

Dunne Ave./East Dunne Ave.

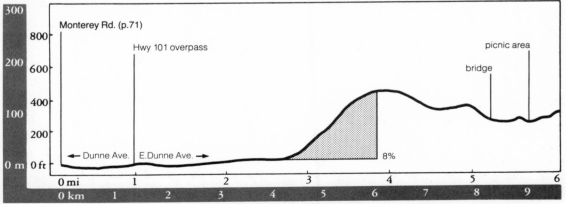

This is the way to Henry Coe State Park. The first few miles outside of Morgan Hill are somewhat developed, with residences, vineyards, a little farmland, and a church. As you ride east, the road narrows quite a bit and begins a winding, oak-shaded climb over steep hills. After the 10th mile or so, the views of the surrounding hills improve as the roadside shade disappears. The climbing is strenuous but enjoyable, particularly during weekdays, when there's less traffic. The descent is a lot of fun anytime.

Dunne Ave./East Dunne Ave. *cont.*

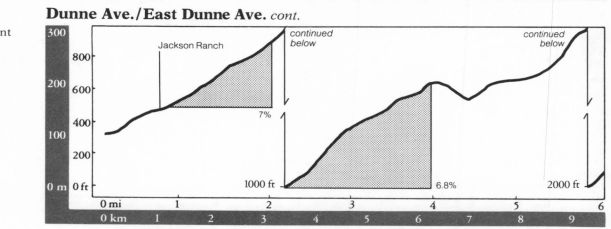

Jackson Ranch

continued below

7%

continued below

1000 ft   6.8%   2000 ft

Dunne Ave./East Dunne Ave. *cont.*

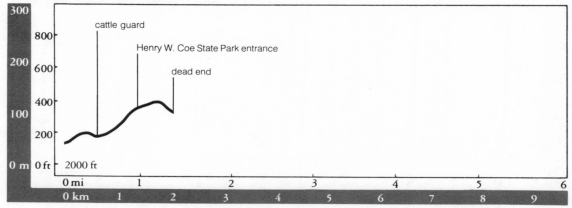

cattle guard

Henry W. Coe State Park entrance

dead end

2000 ft

Edmundson Ave.

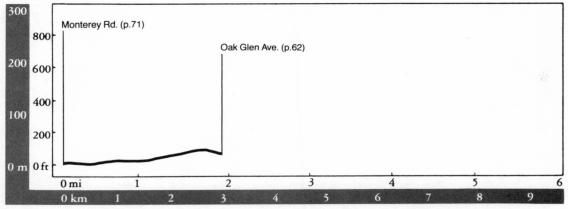

This is a narrow farm road. It travels past ranches, vineyards, and a community park, and meets Oak Glen Ave. at its western end. Light traffic.

Gist Rd.

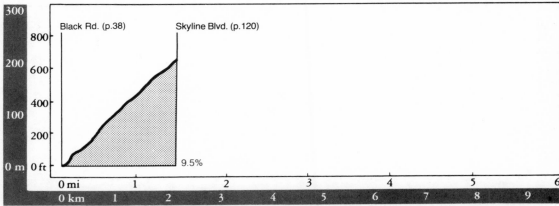

A really skinny road with a rough and abrasive surface. It snakes up the hills through a forest of oaks and madrones between Black Rd. and Skyline Blvd. The car traffic is extremely light—probably 98% of it is from people who live on this road, and the other 2% from people who are off course. It's a steep, very pretty, and interesting road for bicyclists.

Hicks Rd.

This is a challenging and beautiful road. From Camden Ave., it closely follows Guadalupe Creek up to and beyond its source at Guadalupe Reservoir. It climbs past steep pastures partially shaded by stands of oak, laurel, maple, and buckeye. The descents on either side are particularly fast, and should be ridden with caution and good technique. The surface is generally fine, and the traffic light.

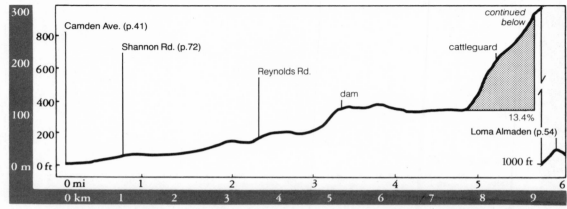

Hicks Rd. *cont.*

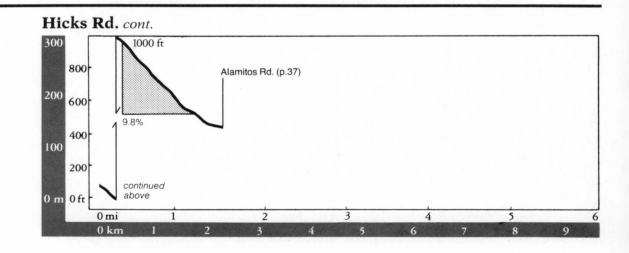

Highway 9 (Saratoga-Los Gatos Rd. / Congress Springs Rd.)

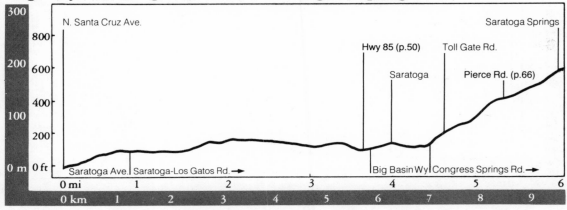

Between Los Gatos and Saratoga, this is a busy road past homes and businesses. From Saratoga to Skyline Blvd, it is much more challenging and enjoyable, winding up the lush hillsides west of town. There's presently a dog training school on this road, so don't panic at the sound of dozens of canines growling and yelping—they're safely caged. The descent back down to Saratoga is narrow, with no shoulder, but is terrific for a skilled rider. With good

Highway 9 *cont.*

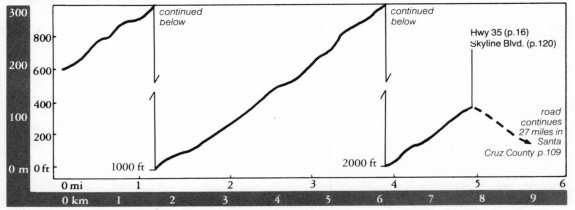

technique, the turns can be taken with minimal use of the brakes, and a fast rider can easily keep up with the car traffic on this section. Less experienced riders may want to avoid this road during evenings and weekends, when traffic is heaviest. The hill has a 6.8% average grade.

Highway 85 (Saratoga-Sunnyvale Rd.)

This is called De Anza Blvd. near Cupertino. It's similar to Stevens Creek Blvd., and just about as unappealing, running through a business district with a lot of traffic. Fortunately, there are bike lanes.

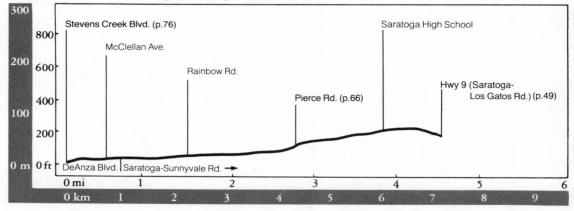

Highway 152 (Hecker Pass Rd.)

This is the most direct route between Watsonville and Gilroy. It handles a lot of cars and is built for it—smooth surface, good shoulder, gentle turns— all things that would make it an excellent road for bicyclists, were it not for the traffic. It travels over mostly undeveloped hills, and provides access to less harried riding on Pole Line Rd. at the top.

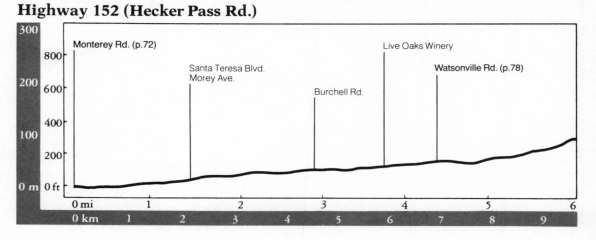

Highway 152 (Hecker Pass Rd.) *cont.*

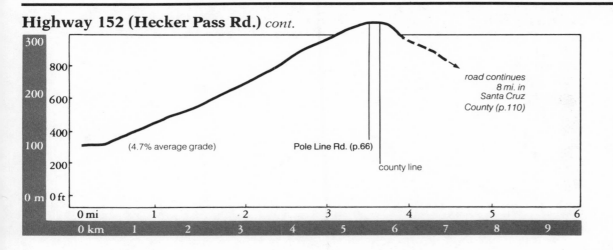

300
800
200
600
400
100
200
0 m   0 ft

(4.7% average grade)

Pole Line Rd. (p.66)

county line

road continues
8 mi. in
Santa Cruz
County (p.110)

0 mi   1   2   3   4   5   6
0 km   1   2   3   4   5   6   7   8   9

Jamison Rd.

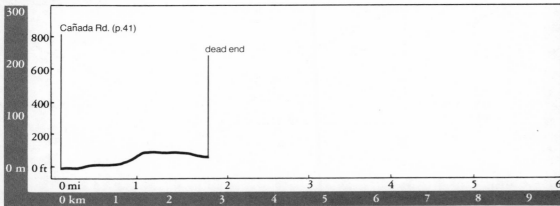

300
800
200
600
400
100
200
0 m   0 ft

Cañada Rd. (p.41)

dead end

0 mi   1   2   3   4   5   6
0 km   1   2   3   4   5   6   7   8   9

This is a narrow and essentially traffic-free tributary of Cañada Rd. It starts in a wide farm valley which it soon climbs above, providing you with a good view. During the wet months, the valley turns green and yellow, and Jamison becomes as pretty a road as you'll ever see. In the summer, one striking feature is the hundreds of ground squirrels running through the grass and popping out of their holes. A dead end, but an absolutely worthwhile diversion.

Kennedy Rd.

The lower, western end of this road is in Los Gatos, and is residential. Towards Shannon Road it is less developed and much better for riding, as it travels over rolling hills and pastures. The road is narrow, with a good surface. You can loop back to Los Gatos on Shannon Rd., or use this as an access road to longer, more strenuous riding on Hicks Rd.

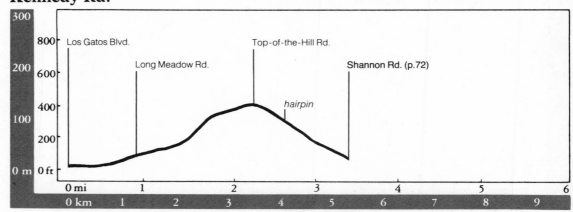

Kincaid Rd.

A very narrow, winding road off Mt. Hamilton Road. It heads down into a densely forested canyon, climbs back up a similar hillside, and dead-ends at a locked gate. Aside from the fact that it's an out-and-back ride, it's an enjoyable, interesting road with almost no motor traffic.

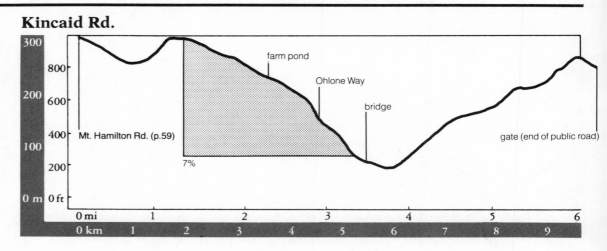

Day Rd.

Cañada Rd.

Las Animas Rd.

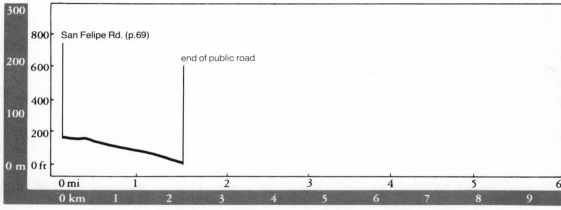

A short, seldom ridden, narrow road, untouched by road crews for many years. From its north end at San Felipe Rd. about half a mile east of Metcalf Rd., it runs south alongside the tiny, wooded Las Animas Creek before becoming private at an entrance to a chemical plant. As short as it is, the riding on it is quiet, beautiful, and perfectly enjoyable. Little motor traffic.

Leavesley Rd.

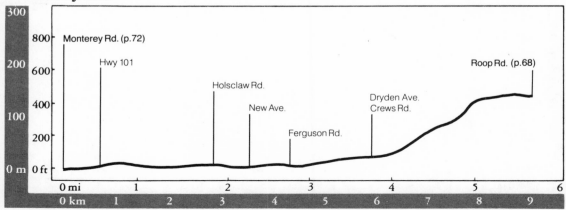

The western part of Leavesley travels a straight course through unspectacular farmland and apricot orchards. North and east of Dryden Avenue it narrows and the surface quality declines, but the overall riding quality improves as it curves and climbs through horse pastures and stands of oak to meet Roop Rd.

Llagas Rd.

This is probably the nicest road in the immediate vicinity of Morgan Hill. The eastern end is residential, and runs through a farm valley that is slowly becoming developed. After about a mile and a half, it changes character and winds up a pretty, partly shaded hill, then descends to Oak Glen Ave. It has a very smooth surface, and little traffic.

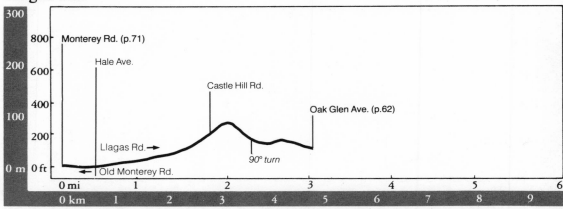

Loma Almaden Rd.

From the summit of Hicks Rd., this road climbs the rim of a deep, chaparral-covered canyon. The intersection with Hicks Rd. is not marked, and it forks near the bottom—stay to the left. From the top, there are spectacular views of Mt. Umunhum and the Los Gatos canyons. It has a good surface, and very little traffic. WARNING: Formerly a restricted federal road, Loma Almaden is still marked as private, and it is possible you will be denied entry.

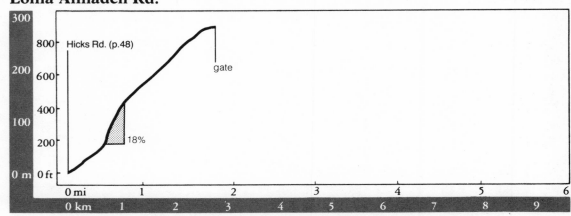

Los Gatos Creek Trail

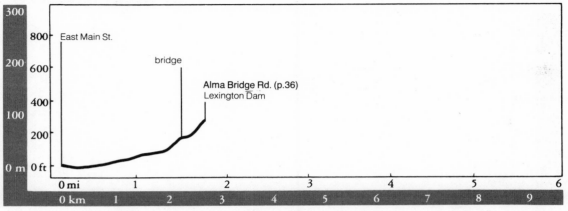

This is an unpaved pathway from Los Gatos to the Lexington Reservoir. No motor vehicles are allowed, and most of the traffic is from runners. Close to Los Gatos, the creek that it parallels has been cemented; a little further on, it's a beautiful wooded creek with a good flow of water throughout the year. When you get to the spillway, cross over it. You'll have to walk up the final climb unless your gears are very low, and your technique refined.

McKean Rd.

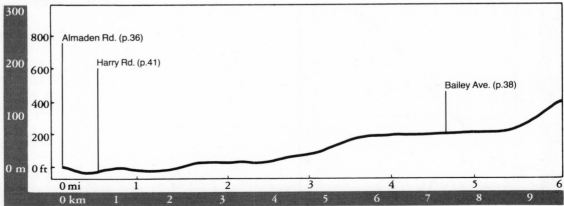

A narrow, mostly shoulderless road through a wide valley bordered by small rolling hills. It passes the Calero Reservoir, and often has a bothersome amount of motor traffic during the summer when the reservoir attracts crowds. It can be an enjoyable road at times of low traffic though; weekdays are always best. Like Uvas Road, which it meets at its southern end, it is often windy and there is no shade.

McKean Rd. *cont.*

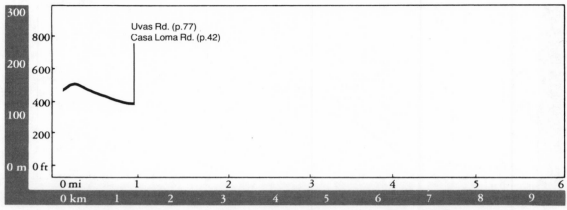

Uvas Rd. (p.77)
Casa Loma Rd. (p.42)

Metcalf Rd.

From its unglamorous beginning at Hwy 101, this road begins a grueling ascent of shadeless, steep pastureland. After you reach the top of the hill, you'll descend a more gentle slope past a great blue heron's pond (easy to miss) and a huge chemical plant (impossible to miss).

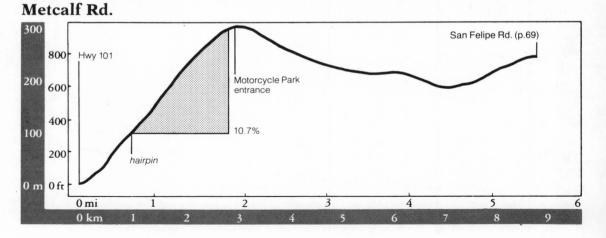

Hwy 101

San Felipe Rd. (p.69)

Motorcycle Park
entrance

10.7%

hairpin

Montebello Rd.

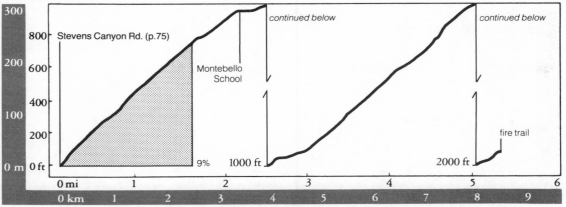

300

800 — Stevens Canyon Rd. (p.75)

200 600 — Montebello
School

100 400 — *continued below* *continued below*

200 — 1000 ft fire trail

0 m 0 ft — 9% 2000 ft

0 mi 1 2 3 4 5 6

0 km 1 2 3 4 5 6 7 8 9

A steep, narrow, dead-end road that climbs from the northern edge of The Fremont Older Open Space Preserve in Stevens Canyon to the eastern border of the Monte Bello Open Space Preserve. It is largely undeveloped, and provides an excellent workout along with a good view of Silicon Valley. At the top, you can ride the fire trail to Page Mill Rd., for an unmatched panorama of the land below. Traffic is light, and the climb averages 7.6%.

Moody Rd.

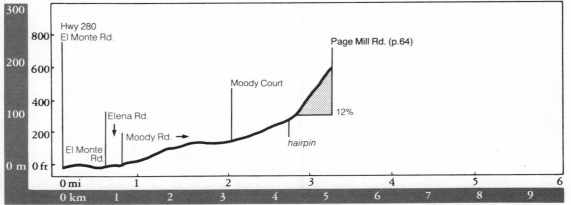

300

800 — Hwy 280
El Monte Rd.

200 600 — Page Mill Rd. (p.64)

100 400 — Moody Court

200 — Elena Rd.
12%
Moody Rd. ➔

0 m 0 ft — El Monte Rd. *hairpin*
El Monte Rd.

0 mi 1 2 3 4 5 6

0 km 1 2 3 4 5 6 7 8 9

This road travels past Foothill College in a semi-rural valley, then narrows considerably and begins a steep, winding, shadeless ascent of chaparral hills above a deep canyon. If you've had enough climbing by the time you reach Page Mill Road, be sure to turn right (north). The traffic is thickest around the college.

Mount Eden Rd.

This is a wooded, narrow, and winding connection between Pierce Rd. and Stevens Canyon Rd. It has a few houses, but the traffic is not bothersome, and there are some enjoyable turns.

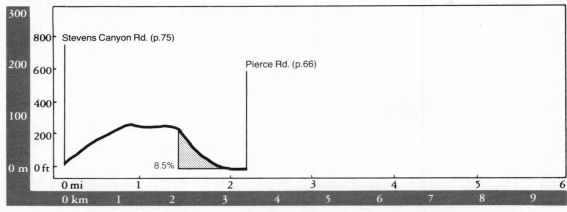

Mount Hamilton Rd. / San Antonio Valley Rd.

This road begins on the outskirts of San Jose, just south of Alum Rock Park at the foot of Mt. Hamilton. The western ascent is dotted with ranch and farmhouses for about the first four miles, changing to oak shaded pastures for the remainder of the climb up to the Lick Observatory. East of the summit it becomes San Antonio Valley Rd., passing Copernicus Peak (4372') in a series of hairpins down to the valley floor. The road levels out along a creek, turning north-

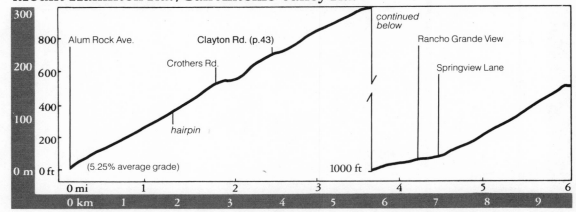

Mount Hamilton Rd. / San Antonio Valley Rd. *cont.*

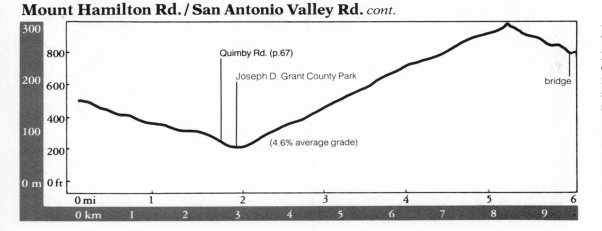

Quimby Rd. (p.67)

Joseph D. Grant County Park

(4.6% average grade)

bridge

ward to meet Del Puerto Rd. There's a tavern there, where you can get water. Beyond the county line it continues in similar character, eventually descending into the southern outskirts of Livermore as Mines Rd. The road is narrow, the surface is generally fine, and there's very little traffic. A strenuous but enjoyable ride; just be sure to bring plenty of food and water, as facilities are minimal.

Mount Hamilton Rd. / San Antonio Valley Rd. *cont.*

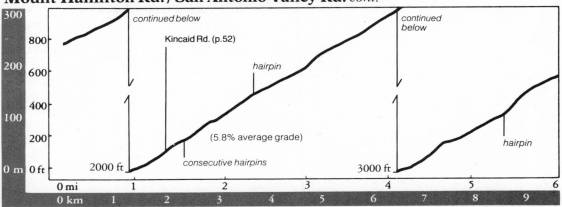

continued below

Kincaid Rd. (p.52)

hairpin

continued below

(5.8% average grade)

2000 ft

consecutive hairpins

3000 ft

hairpin

Mount Hamilton Rd. / San Antonio Valley Rd. *cont.*

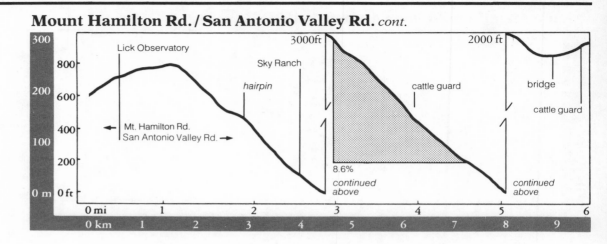

Mount Hamilton Rd. / San Antonio Valley Rd. *cont.*

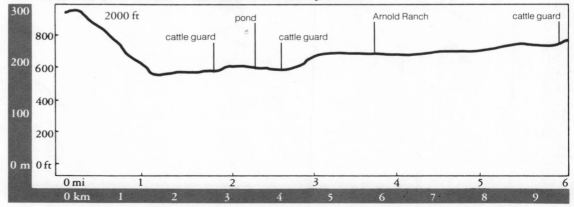

Mount Hamilton Rd. / San Antonio Valley Rd. *cont.*

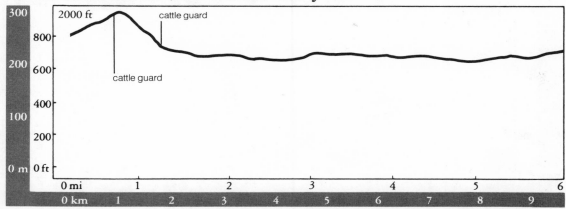

Mount Hamilton Rd. / San Antonio Valley Rd. *cont.*

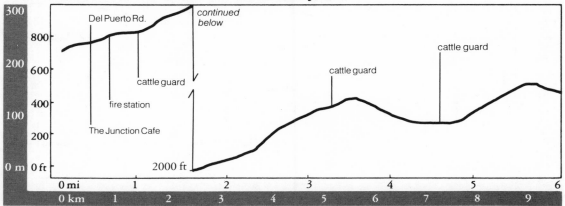

Mount Hamilton Rd. / San Antonio Valley Rd. *cont.*

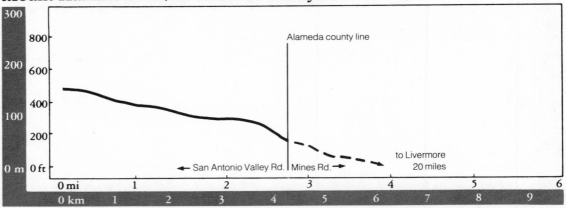

Oak Glen Ave.

This is a narrow road with a gravel shoulder that travels among gently rolling hills west of Morgan Hill. The traffic moves at a fairly high speed, and it tends to get windy out there, but Oak Glen can be useful as part of a nice mid-week ride along with several of the other roads in the area, such as Uvas, Watsonville, Sycamore, Llagas, Willow Springs, and Edmundson.

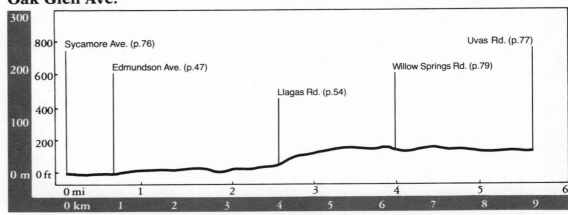

Old Page Mill Rd.

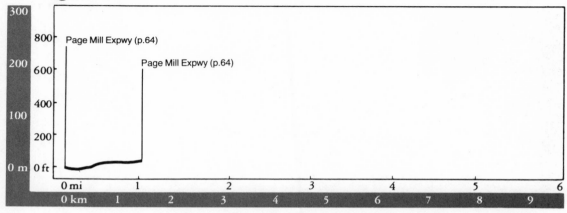

A quiet and pleasant diversion off the Page Mill Expressway. It gives you the feeling of being much further away from civilization than you really are.

Old Santa Cruz Highway

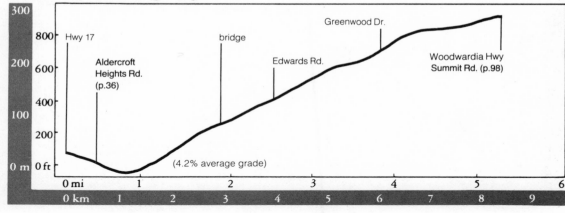

This is a narrow, curvy, wooded residential road between Hwy 17 and Summit Rd. The road surface is fine, and the traffic is moderate.

This road begins as the Page Mill Expressway, a wide urban thoroughfare. Page Mill Road officially starts west of Hwy 280. After travelling over gentle, rural terrain for about a mile and a half, it begins a killer seven mile ascent up the eastern side of the Santa Cruz Mountains through a beautiful forest of oaks, madrones, douglas fir, maples, and manzanita. If you look around, you'll see the distant hills and canyons as you climb above them. The upper-

Page Mill Rd.

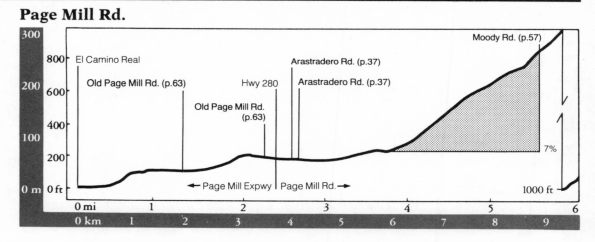

most portion is more open, but what it lacks in shade it will often make up for in fog. The road surface is fine, the traffic is moderate most of the time, and the descent is a blast.

Page Mill Rd. *cont.*

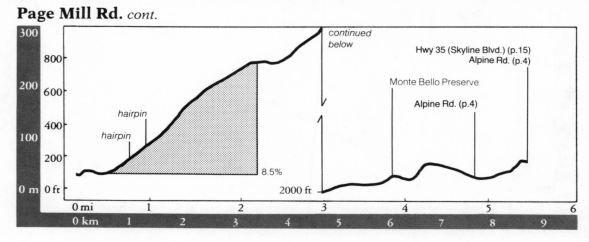

Penitencia Creek Rd.

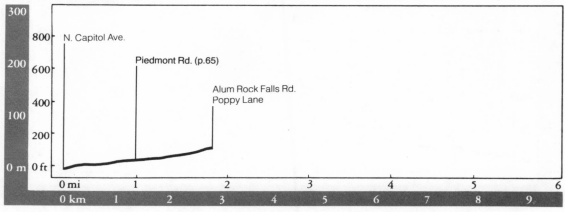

The western half of this road is smooth and residential. The eastern section enters Alum Rock Falls State Park, winding gently between a hillside and a creek; it ends at a parking lot near the Visitor's Center.

Piedmont Rd.

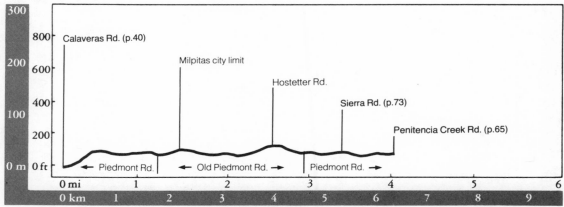

This route travels along the eastern outskirts of Milpitas. It's primarily a residential road, although there is a short undeveloped portion near the southern border of town. Immediately to the east are the Los Buellis Hills, and Piedmont/Old Piedmont serves best as an access road to excellent riding in these hills on Sierra and Felter Roads.

Pierce Rd.

This road travels between a poor bicyling road (Hwy 85) and an excellent one (Hwy 9, Congress Springs). The north-eastern portion is narrow, passing homes and small vine-yards. The hill is a more rural area, and is the home of the Paul Masson Winery. Traffic is mod-erate, and the road surface is generally fine.

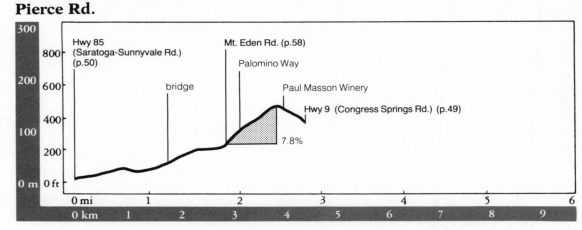

Pole Line Rd.

This is a pretty and interesting road between the summit of Mt. Madonna Rd. and the top of Hwy 152. It's the main route through Mt. Madonna County Park and the traffic can be thick at times, but it's still a nice road. A narrow road, it travels through shaded hills, past several picnic areas and a deer pen which presently houses some pretty strange looking deer. As the profile indicates, there is one very steep section where you may end up pushing your bike.

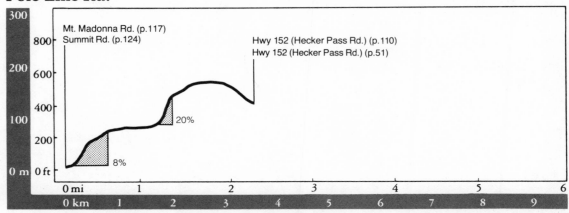

Jamison Rd.

San Felipe Rd.

Quimby Rd.

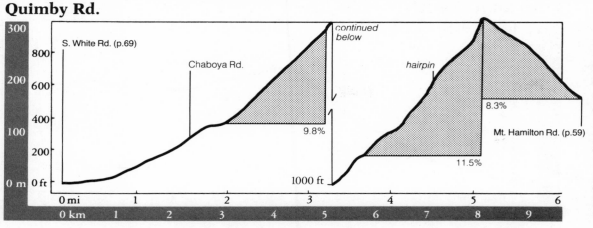

Here's a tough one. After two miles of housing developments, Quimby Rd. begins a relentless and almost shadeless climb over the foothills of Mt. Hamilton. After several minutes of climbing, you'll get a view of San Jose. Continuing upwards, you'll pass a few scattered ranches on your way to the summit. From this point, it's a fun, twisting descent into Joseph D. Grant County Park, and Mt. Hamilton Rd. Little traffic, and the surface is fine.

Redwood Retreat Rd.

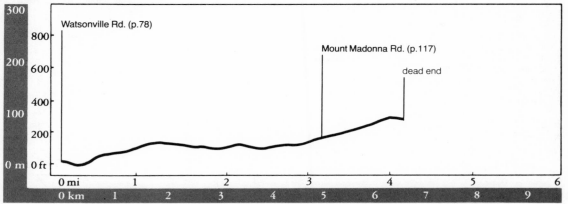

This begins as a quiet rural road that branches off from Watsonville Rd., about 2 miles east of Mt. Madonna County Park. It passes small pastures, a few houses, and travels alongside Little Arthur Creek under the shade of redwoods. A narrow road, with a decent surface and light traffic.

From its western end at New
Ave. northeast of Gilroy, Roop
Rd. travels through farmland,
and then winds and climbs over
open pastures to Coyote Lake
Rd. East of there, it is called
Gilroy Hot Springs Rd., and
winds along a gravelly creek,
shaded by oaks. A truly
fantastic loop can be made by
turning on to Cañada and
following it back around
towards Gilroy. The traffic is
typically light during the mid-
dle of the week, heavier on

Roop Rd./Gilroy Hot Springs Rd.

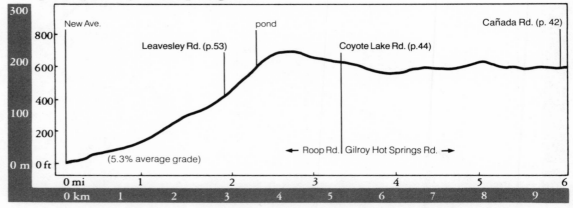

weekends. WARNING: Gilroy
Hot Springs has recently been
declared private beyond
Cañada. You may be denied
entry.

Roop Rd./Gilroy Hot Springs Rd. *cont.*

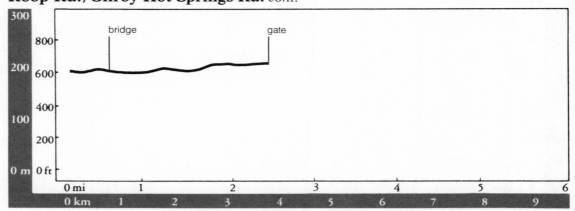

San Felipe Rd.

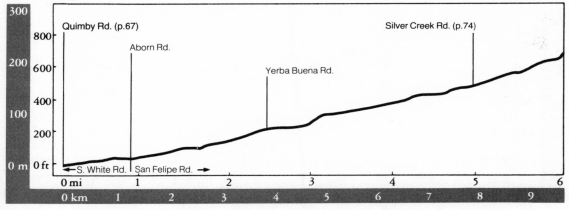

The lower, northern end of this road travels over farmland which is in the process of being taken over by housing developments. It is wide, with heavy traffic. Shortly after Aborn Rd. it narrows considerably and becomes rural, running southeast between a hillside and a wooded creek. The most enjoyable portion begins at the junction of Metcalf Rd. (spelled "Medcalf" on the sign), overlooking the beautiful pastures of San Felipe Valley. It's a narrow stretch

San Felipe Rd. *cont.*

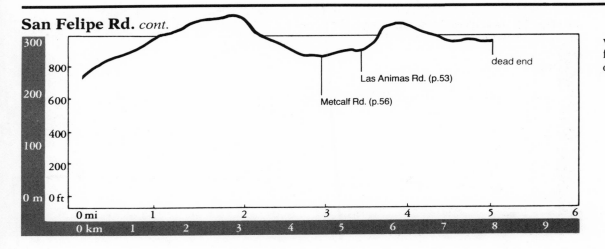

with great turns and little traffic. It dead-ends a few miles east of Mt. Misery.

Santa Teresa Blvd./Monterey Rd.

Don't ride this unless you have to. While much of the road passes through farmland, there's a lot of high-speed traffic, and no scenery interesting enough to distract your attention from all the cars. Although it does have bike lanes, the quality of riding is very low, and your cycling hours are much better spent elsewhere.

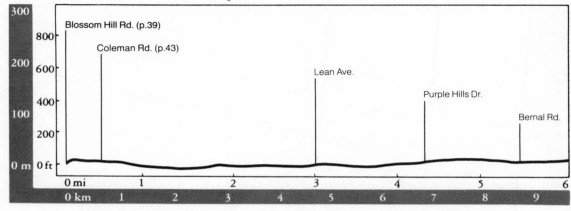

Santa Teresa Blvd./Monterey Rd. *cont.*

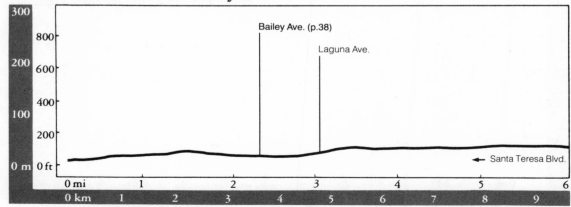

Santa Teresa Blvd./Monterey Rd. *cont.*

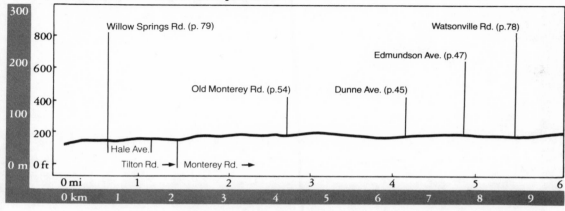

Willow Springs Rd. (p. 79)

Watsonville Rd. (p.78)

Edmundson Ave. (p.47)

Old Monterey Rd. (p.54)

Dunne Ave. (p.45)

Hale Ave.

Tilton Rd. ➜   Monterey Rd. ➜

Santa Teresa Blvd./Monterey Rd. *cont.*

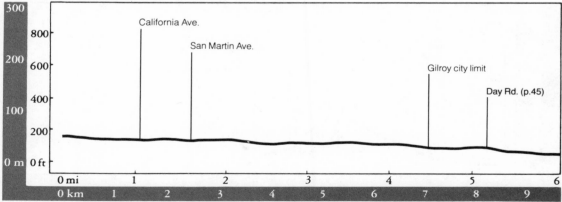

California Ave.

San Martin Ave.

Gilroy city limit

Day Rd. (p.45)

Santa Teresa Blvd./Monterey Rd. *cont.*

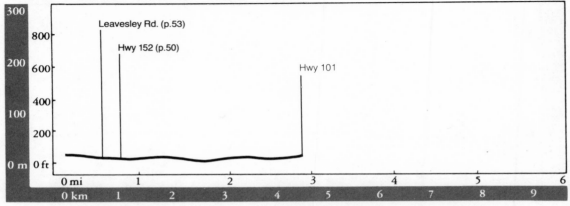

Shannon Rd.

This is a residential road near Los Gatos. The eastern portion is more rural, climbing and descending past horse pastures, stables, and ranches on its way to Hicks Rd. It's a nice road with a decent surface, light traffic, and ample shade.

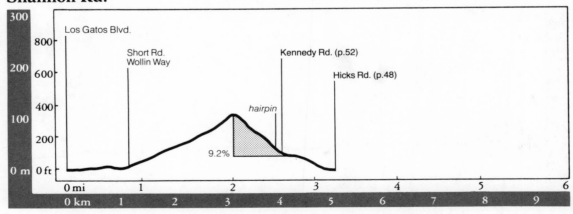

Sierra Rd./Felter Rd.

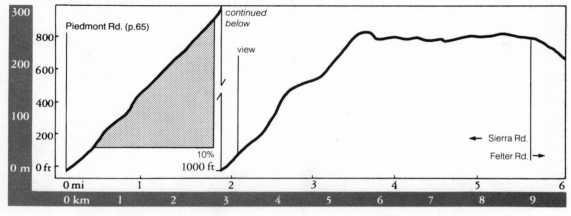

These roads comprise a hilly, narrow, shadeless loop over the Los Buellis Hills, east of Milpitas and south of Calaveras Reservoir. The terrain is strenuous, and in the warmer months you'll need to bring sufficient water, but the riding is excellent. There are superior distant views, the nearby landscape is interesting, and there is very little motor traffic.

Sierra Rd./Felter Rd. *cont.*

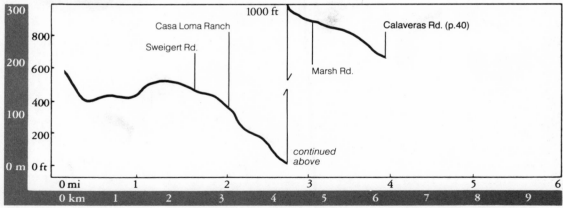

Silver Creek Rd.

A narrow road with a gravel shoulder and a somewhat rough surface. It curves and climbs over rolling, oak-shaded pastureland southeast of San Jose. The traffic is fairly light.

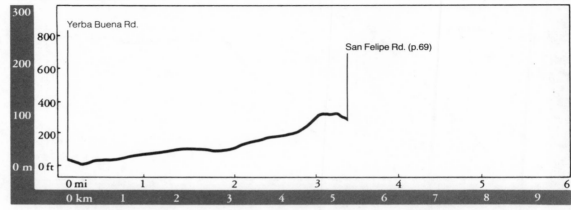

Soda Springs Rd.

To ride this road, you will have to want an extra-hard workout and be willing to go somewhat out of your way. From its beginning at Alma Bridge Rd. on the eastern shore of Lexington Reservoir, it climbs the side of a deep canyon, through a beautiful, dense forest of oaks. The narrow surface is rough in some places and slick in others, but it poses no major problems. Descending this road is a lot of fun, but the many sharp turns demand both constant attention and good technique.

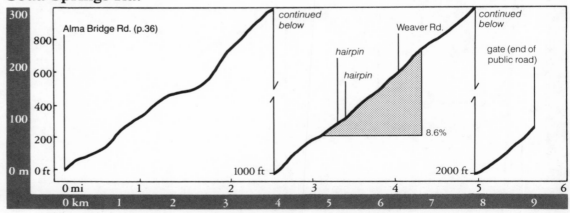

Stevens Canyon Rd.

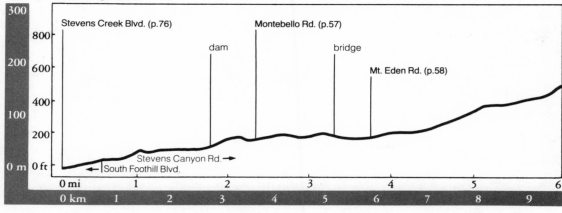

This begins as South Foothill Blvd. at Stevens Creek Blvd. It heads south, changes names, and travels alongside the hills above Stevens Creek Reservoir near the Fremont Older Open Space Preserve. After about 3 miles it narrows significantly and follows a small creek in the shade of maples, oaks, and madrones. This portion is rather rough, and takes you over the creek several times on small bridges. The final time the road crosses the creek, there's

Stevens Canyon Rd. *cont.*

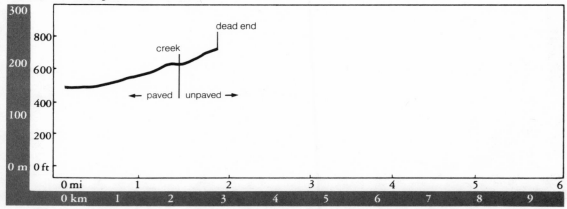

no bridge, and you ride right through the water—providing it's sufficiently shallow. Beyond this last crossing, it's unpaved. The traffic is moderate alongside the reservoir; light as it follows the creek.

Stevens Creek Blvd.

A six lane road that passes through a business district, Stevens Creek Blvd. is useful only as a connector. There are bike lanes to separate you from the hordes of motorists on your way to better riding somewhere else.

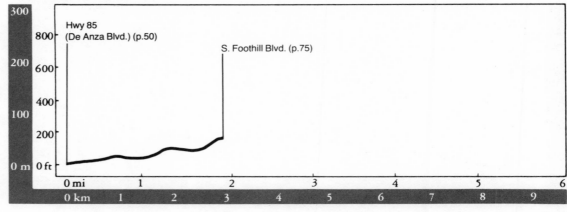

Sycamore Ave.

A quiet, rural road south of Morgan Hill. The steeper section is the most interesting and enjoyable, climbing over pastureland dotted with oak trees. The traffic is light, and the road has an adequate surface but no shoulder.

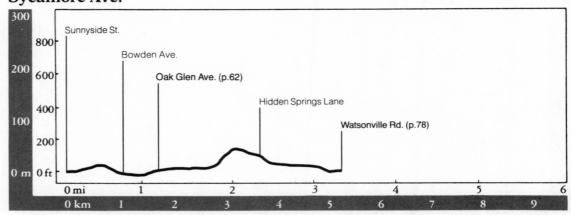

Uvas Rd.

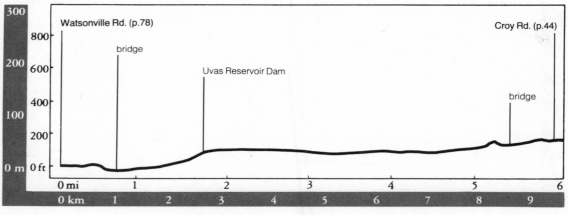

This is a narrow, fairly straight road that travels through the reservoir country west of Morgan Hill. It's useful for any loop ride you might want to construct in the area, as it connects several other interesting roads. Although there are no steep grades, what looks like an easy ride can be made more difficult by the wind, which seems to whip up with regularity in these parts. The weekend traffic can be annoying, due to heavy recreational use of Calero, Ches-

Uvas Rd. *cont.*

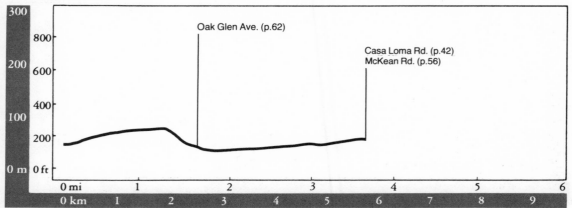

bro, and Uvas Reservoirs, and there's no shade.

This is a narrow rural road that carries a lot of traffic. As it approaches Santa Teresa Blvd., it widens, and the road becomes residential with even more traffic. It does, however, connect to more enjoyable roads—Redwood Retreat Rd. in particular.

Watsonville Rd.

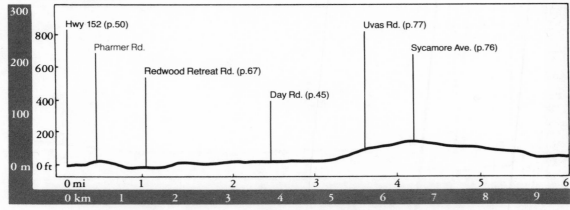

Watsonville Rd. *cont.*

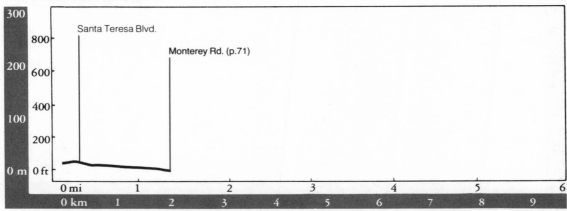

Willow Springs Rd.

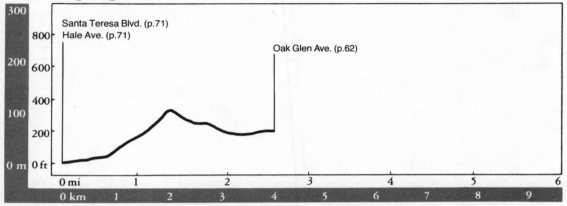

Santa Teresa Blvd. (p.71)
Hale Ave. (p.71)

Oak Glen Ave. (p.62)

This road begins by passing farmhouses and planted fields, then climbs over open pasture-land before winding back down into the shade of oaks near Chesbro Reservoir. It has a decent surface, and light traffic.

Mt. Madonna Rd.

Santa Cruz County

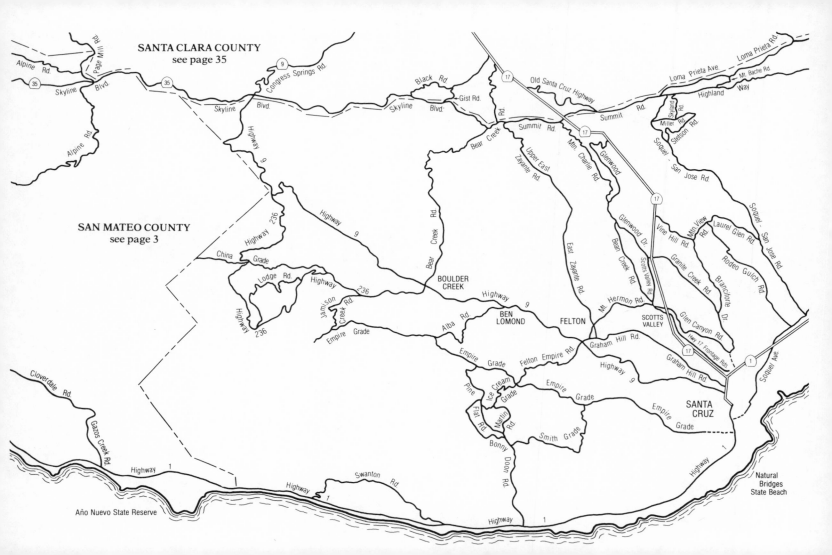

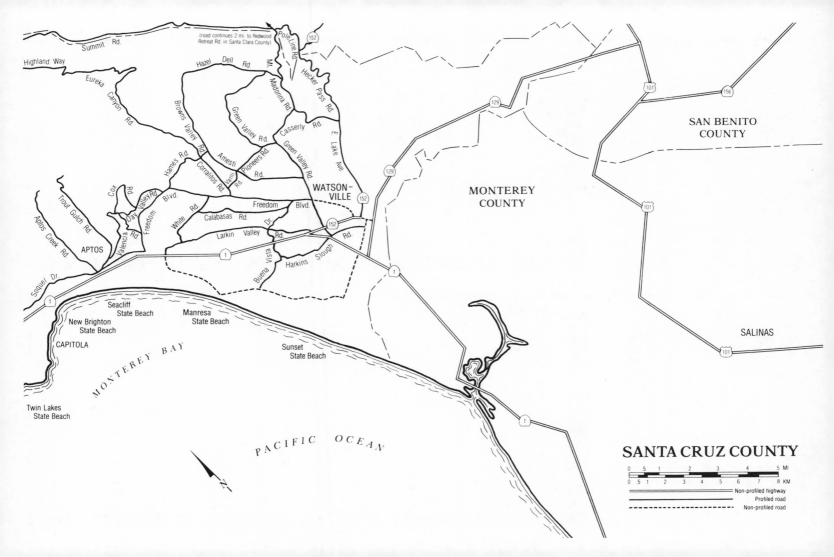

Summit Rd.

Highland Way

Eureka Canyon Rd.

(road continues 2 mi. to Redwood Retreat Rd. in Santa Clara County)

Hazel Dell Rd.

Pole Line Rd.

152

Madonna Rd.

Hecker Pass Rd.

Casserly Rd.

Green Valley Rd.

Browns Valley Rd.

Green Valley Rd.

E. Lake Ave.

Amesti Rd.

Pioneers Rd.

Corralitos Rd.

Nash Rd.

Hames Rd.

WATSON-VILLE

152

Cox Rd.

Day Valley Rd.

Freedom Blvd.

White Rd.

Freedom Blvd.

129

Trout Gulch Rd.

Valencia Rd.

Calabasas Rd.

Freedom Dr.

152

Rd.

129

Aptos Creek Rd.

APTOS

Larkin Valley Rd.

Buena Vista Dr.

Harkins Slough

152

1

MONTEREY COUNTY

101

156

SAN BENITO COUNTY

Soquel Dr.

1

Seacliff State Beach

Manresa State Beach

1

101

New Brighton State Beach

CAPITOLA

Sunset State Beach

101

SALINAS

MONTEREY BAY

1

Twin Lakes State Beach

PACIFIC OCEAN

N

SANTA CRUZ COUNTY

0 .5 1   2   3   4   5 MI
0 .5 1 2   3   4   5   6   7   8 KM

————————— Non-profiled highway
————————— Profiled road
– – – – – – Non-profiled road

Alba Rd.

This is one of the most difficult short climbs in the Santa Cruz Mountains. It does, however, travel through a thick redwood forest which provides you with shade as you grunt to the top. The surface is rather rough in places, though it's easy to avoid the worst spots. The traffic is light, but on roads like this it's particularly unnerving to be passed by cars. Descending Alba Rd. isn't great fun, but rather a matter of constantly arresting your speed and looking forward to the bottom.

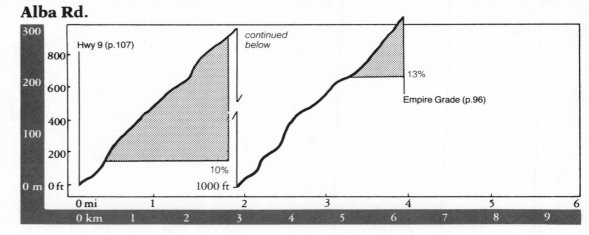

Amesti Rd.

The southern portion of this road is rural, passing through orchards and farms. Toward Browns Valley Rd. it becomes somewhat more residential. It has a fine surface and light traffic, and is a much less busy alternative to Freedom Blvd.

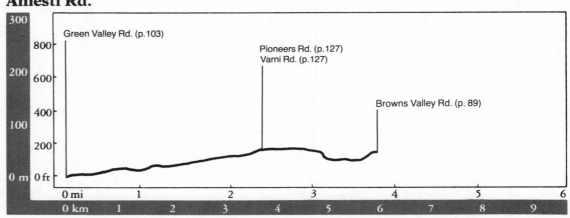

Aptos Creek Rd.

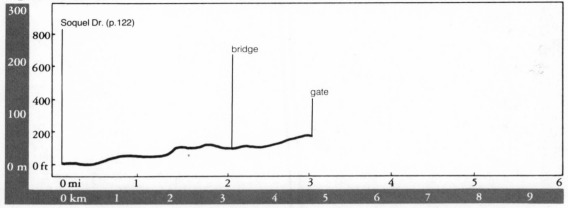

This road takes you from the town of Aptos into the Forest of Nisene Marks State Park. Except for a short paved section near town, it's a narrow dirt and gravel road running alongside Aptos Creek in a dense forest of redwoods. It stops at the southern end of a hiking trail. There isn't much traffic on weekdays, but there is more on weekends, and it's particularly bothersome as the cars kick up a lot of slow-settling dust.

Bean Creek Rd.

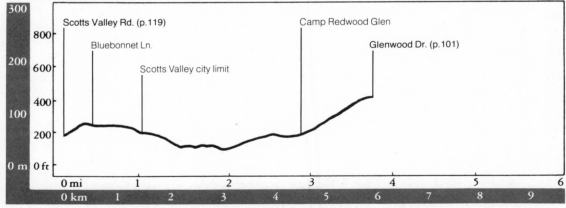

This is a very pretty backwoods residential road. It parallels Bean Creek for most of its length, and is shaded by pines, maples, laurels, and redwoods. It has a very smooth surface, great turns, and light traffic. The lower portion is in Scotts Valley.

The lower, flatter portion of this road, near Boulder Creek, is residential. The upper part winds through a pine and redwood forest, and the western slope from Skyline Blvd. down provides what may be the most exhilarating descent in Santa Cruz County. The surface is new, and the turns are perfectly smooth and well-banked. There are a couple of hairpins, but the majority of the turns can be taken at a good speed, with minimal use of the brakes. The motor

Bear Creek Rd.

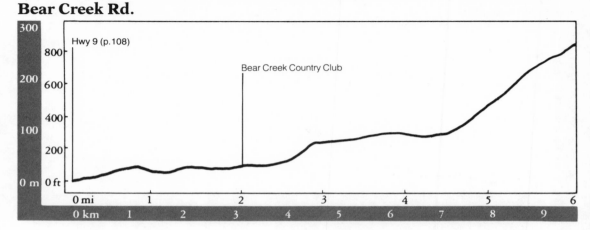

traffic can be bothersome at times, but there's an ample shoulder to escape to when the cars zoom by. Like Bear Creek Rd. near Orinda in Alameda County, this is a nice road for bicyclists.

Bear Creek Rd. *cont.*

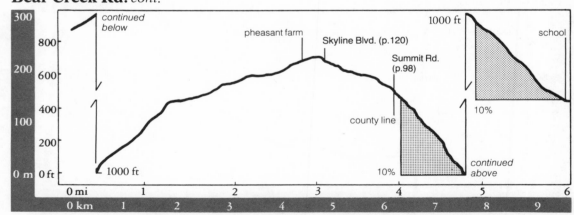

Bear Creek Rd. *cont.*

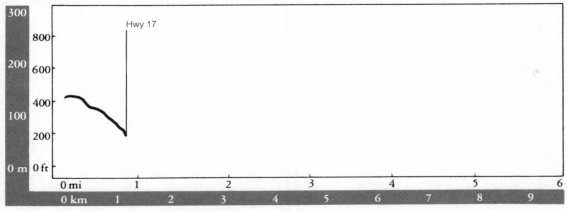

Bonny Doon Rd.

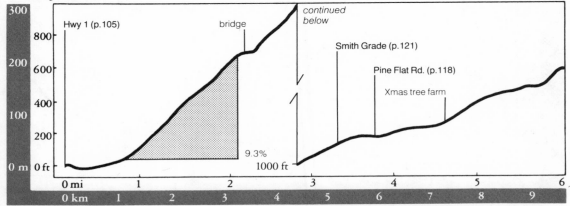

This is a strenuous climb and a speedy descent. From the coast, Bonny Doon Rd. travels up a brushy canyon, then climbs an unshaded hillside out of the canyon to the tiny settlement of Bonny Doon. It jogs left at the junction of Pine Flat Rd., looping up to meet Pine Flat Rd. again above Ice Cream Grade. The road surface is good, with little traffic.

Bonny Doon Rd. *cont.*

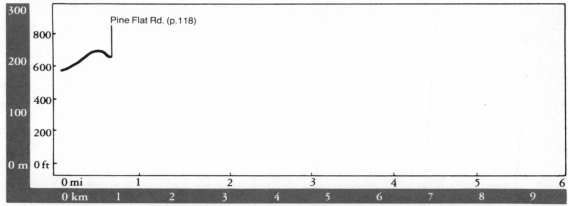

Pine Flat Rd. (p.118)

Branciforte Dr. / Vine Hill Rd.

This is a residential country road northeast of Santa Cruz. It follows Branciforte Creek, and is partially shaded by redwoods. North of Mountain View Rd. its name changes to Vine Hill Rd. The road surface is fine, and the traffic is moderate.

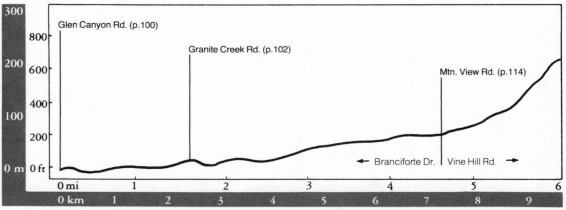

Glen Canyon Rd. (p.100)

Granite Creek Rd. (p.102)

Mtn. View Rd. (p.114)

← Branciforte Dr. | Vine Hill Rd. →

Branciforte Dr. / Vine Hill Rd. *cont.*

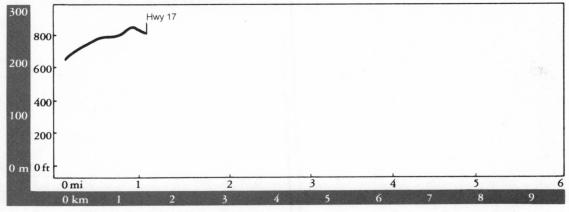

Browns Valley Rd. / Hazel Dell Rd.

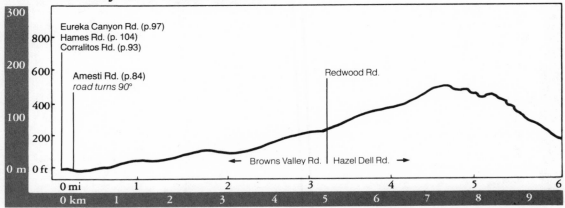

Browns Valley Rd. is quiet and beautiful, travelling through a lush forest of redwoods. It becomes Hazel Dell Rd. at Redwood Rd., and the scenery changes to flat pastureland for the last mile or so. Both roads are narrow, with light traffic.

Browns Valley Rd. / Hazel Dell Rd. *cont.*

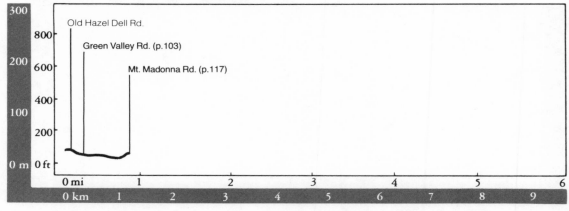

Buena Vista Dr.

The eastern portion of this is residential and unexciting. The more enjoyable western portion travels over relatively undeveloped farmland, and has a few fun turns and easy rolls. It's narrow, with light to moderate traffic.

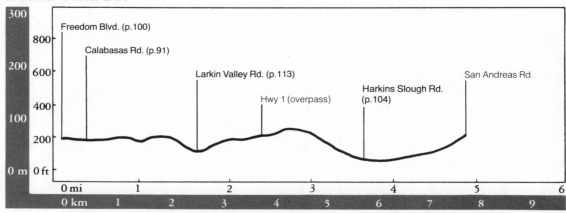

Calabasas Rd.

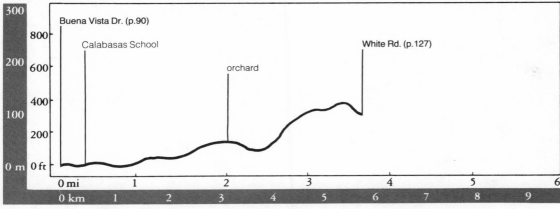

This is one of the nicer roads in the Watsonville area, and in combination with White Rd., Larkin Valley Rd., and Buena Vista Dr., forms a pretty, enjoyable loop. As it heads northwest, it travels past rolling orchards and farmland, then winds up through a stand of eucalyptus trees to meet White Rd. The road surface is fine, and the traffic is light.

Casserly Rd.

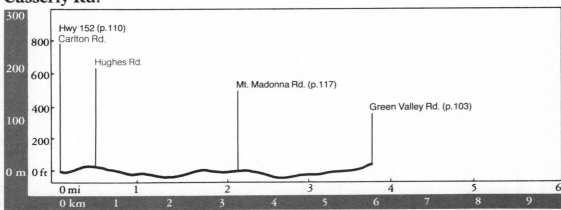

This is a narrow, flat farm road with a smooth surface. It has light, mostly local traffic, and is a good warm-up road for Mt. Madonna Rd., which it intersects.

China Grade

This is a very narrow road with an abrasive surface and many large potholes. It winds up over a steep hillside shaded by redwoods on the eastern edge of Big Basin Redwoods State Park, crosses Hwy 236 again further north, and continues climbing through a sparse forest mixed with chaparral. The pavement eventually peters out, and it continues on as a dirt road until the dead end. A strenuous, beautiful road with very little traffic.

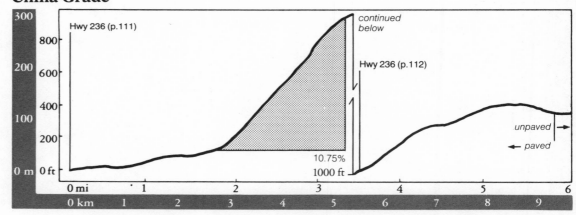

China Grade *cont.*

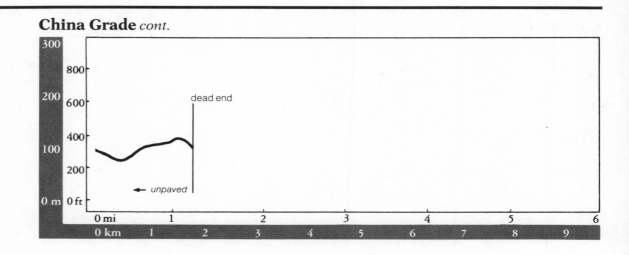

Corralitos Rd.

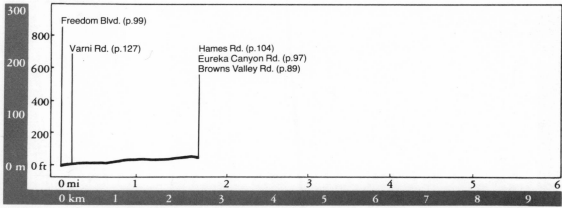

This is a residential road that travels through apple orchards in a wide valley between Freedom Blvd. and the town of Corralitos. The most prominent landmark is the Corralitos Market & Sausage Company. Traffic is light.

Cox Rd.

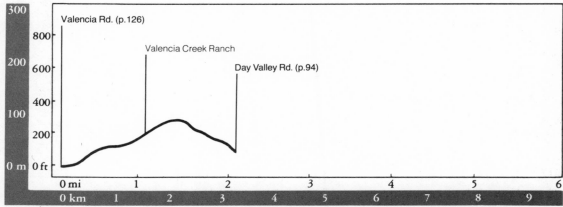

A quiet rural road northeast of Aptos. It passes a few orchards, then climbs up and curves around them to meet Day Valley Rd. Light traffic, and rather pretty scenery.

Day Valley Rd.

This is a short, narrow road with an abrasive surface. It passes by houses and orchards, and travels through oak, bay, and eucalyptus trees. The turns are fun and the traffic is local and light.

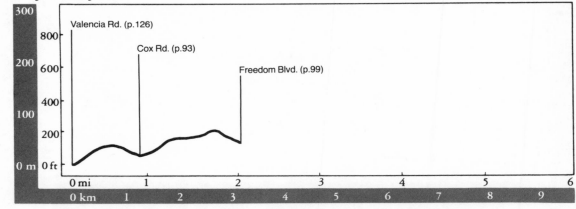

East Zayante Rd.

A beautiful road. The lower portion of it is narrow, has a very small, sometimes nonexistent shoulder, and travels a gently winding course into the mountains northeast of Felton. Above the town of Zayante—indicated primarily by the Zayante Store—the road narrows even more, and begins the long, winding ascent to Summit Rd., broken only by a brief respite at mile 7.5. The upper portion has a rough surface, and generally light traffic. A few commuters

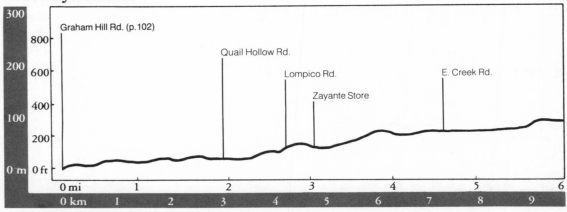

East Zayante Rd. *cont.*

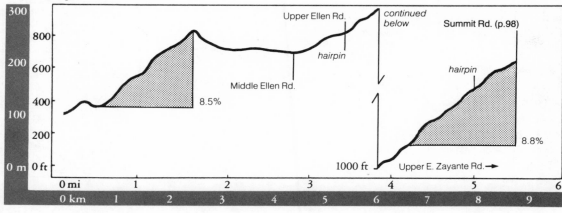

use it in the evening, and riders should use extra caution at this time of day.

Empire Grade

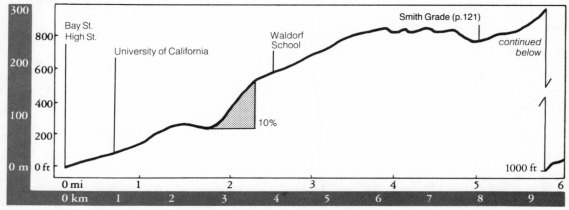

Empire Grade is a lot like Skyline Blvd. in that it travels parallel to the coast on a forested ridge, and intersects many other fun and useful roads. Although the climbing is continuous, it isn't very steep, and the descent can be ridden without much braking. The surface is fine, and while the commute-hour can be a bit bothersome, traffic isn't bad at other times as most drivers prefer Hwy 9 to the east.

Empire Grade *cont.*

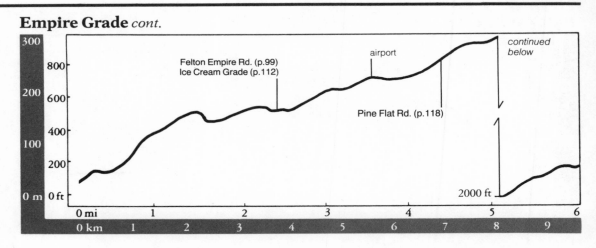

continued below

Felton Empire Rd. (p.99)
Ice Cream Grade (p.112)

airport

Pine Flat Rd. (p.118)

2000 ft

Empire Grade *cont.*

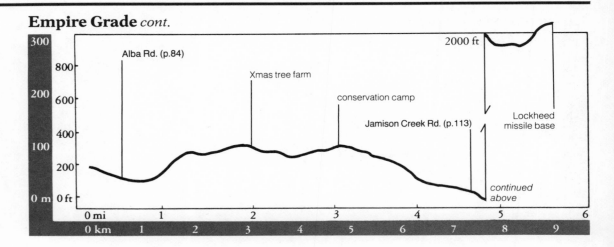

2000 ft

Alba Rd. (p.84)

Xmas tree farm

conservation camp

Jamison Creek Rd. (p.113)

Lockheed missile base

continued above

Eureka Canyon Rd. / Highland Way / Summit Rd.

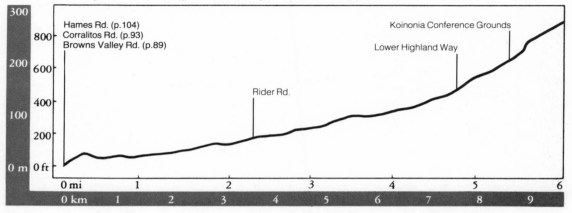

Hames Rd. (p.104)
Corralitos Rd. (p.93)
Browns Valley Rd. (p.89)

Rider Rd.

Koinonia Conference Grounds

Lower Highland Way

Eureka Canyon begins in the town of Corralitos as a narrow, wooded residential road. As the houses thin out, it becomes a beautiful, winding road that follows Corralitos Creek up a lush, shady canyon. The roadside trees are mostly redwoods, oaks, and madrones, and the steep hillsides are bursting with ferns and an assortment of wildflowers. Near the top, it becomes Highland Way, a narrow, rough-surfaced road bordered primarily by oaks, pines, and

Eureka Canyon Rd. / Highland Way / Summit Rd. *cont.*

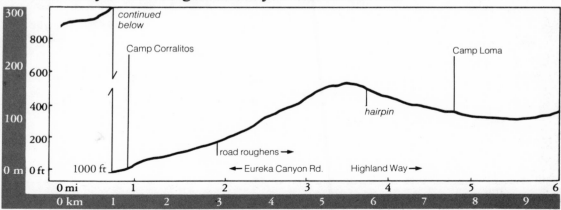

continued below

Camp Corralitos

Camp Loma

hairpin

road roughens →

← Eureka Canyon Rd.

Highland Way →

1000 ft

chaparral. Summit Road east of Hwy 17 is lightly developed. The traffic here travels fast, and although there's a small shoulder, it can be bothersome. West of Hwy 17, however, Summit encourages a relaxed pace—it's a winding road slightly over one lane wide, shaded by buckeyes and oaks.

Eureka Canyon Rd. / Highland Way / Summit Rd. *cont.*

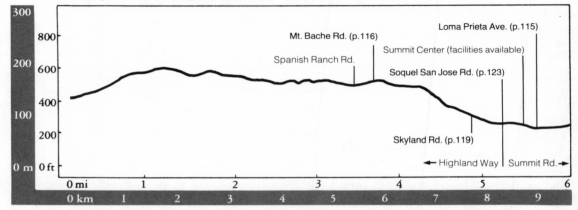

Eureka Canyon Rd. / Highland Way / Summit Rd. *cont.*

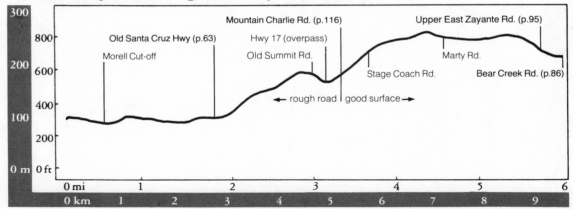

Loma Prieta Ave.

Mt. Bache Rd.

Felton Empire Rd.

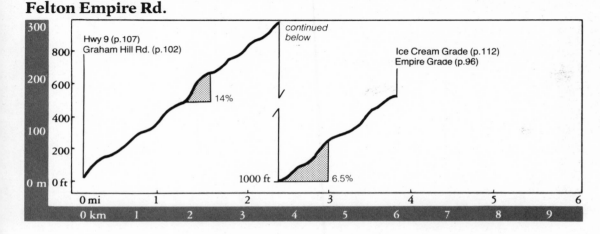

This road was sensibly named after the town where it begins and the road where it ends. It's a beautiful, well-shaded road through the densely forested hills of Henry Cowell Redwoods State Park. The surface is adequate, the traffic is fairly light, and the riding is strenuous, exciting and beautiful. It has an average grade of 8%.

Freedom Blvd.

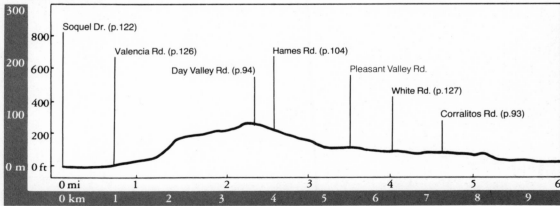

This is the main freeway alternative between Aptos and Watsonville. It travels through small business districts and farmland, has lots of traffic, and is far more useful than it is fun. There are bike lanes for most of its length.

Freedom Blvd. *cont.*

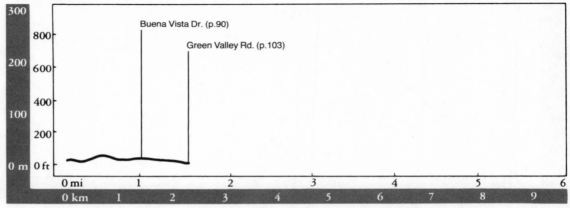

Glen Canyon Rd.

A narrow rural road between De Laveaga Park and Scotts Valley. It passes a few farmhouses and horse pastures along the way, and has a fairly light flow of traffic that increases noticeably during commute hours.

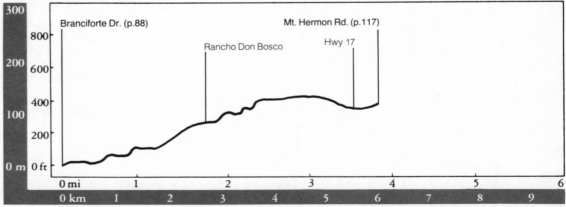

Glenwood Dr.

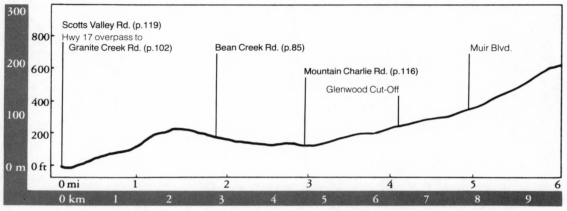

Scotts Valley Rd. (p.119)
Hwy 17 overpass to
Granite Creek Rd. (p.102)

Bean Creek Rd. (p.85)

Mountain Charlie Rd. (p.116)

Glenwood Cut-Off

Muir Blvd.

This is a beautiful road with excellent riding, which has the dubious distinction of beginning and ending right on Hwy 17. Consequently, few bicyclists ride it north of Mtn. Charlie Rd., despite the fact that this section is the nicest part of the road. This upper portion has a smooth surface broken by straight, full-width cracks, but these don't pose much of a problem, as they're predictable and spread out. It curves through the shade of tall maples, redwoods, and

Glenwood Dr. *cont*.

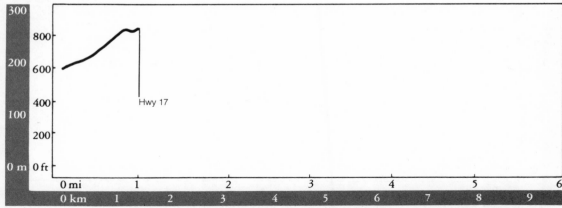

Hwy 17

oaks, and is fun to ride. The lower portion is somewhat residential, and has a rougher surface. Overall, the traffic is light, but slightly thicker at commute times.

Graham Hill Rd.

This is a busy alternative to the freeway between Santa Cruz and Felton. It passes through semi-developed hillsides, and has no aesthetic appeal. It does have bike lanes, however, and is a slightly more direct route between these two towns than Hwy 9, to the west. Utilitarian, but not particularly enjoyable.

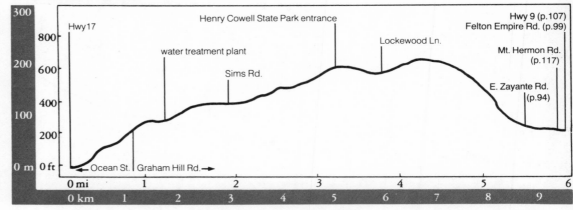

Granite Creek Rd.

This is one of the prettiest roads I've ridden, despite the fact that it isn't way out in the boondocks. It rolls and winds gently through a shaded forest of redwoods, oaks, and madrones, alongside hills covered with ferns, poison oak, and occasional wildflowers. It also parallels a creek, the bed of which actually is partly composed of granite. The traffic is light enough and the surface smooth enough to allow you to concentrate on the sights.

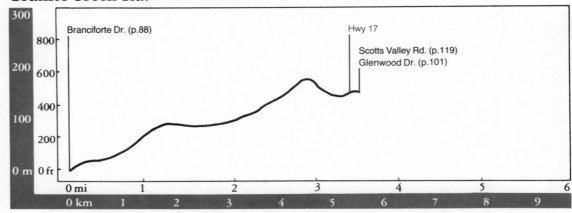

Green Valley Rd.

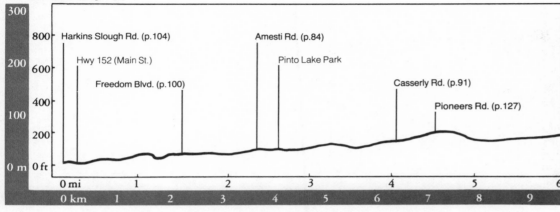

While the southern end of this road is developed, the rest of it travels over agricultural land, and is much more pleasant to ride. It meets up with Hazel Dell Rd. just southwest of Mt. Madonna County Park. While the traffic on this road is generally light, it is thickest near Freedom Blvd.

Green Valley Rd. *cont.*

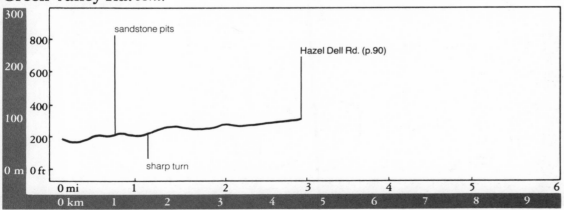

Hames Rd.

A narrow, quiet residential road east of Aptos and north of Watsonville that travels past several apple orchards. A little more than half a mile from the western end, Pleasant Valley Road interferes with its continuity for about 30 yards.

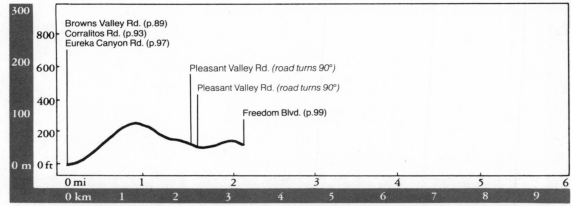

Browns Valley Rd. (p.89)
Corralitos Rd. (p.93)
Eureka Canyon Rd. (p.97)
Pleasant Valley Rd. *(road turns 90°)*
Pleasant Valley Rd. *(road turns 90°)*
Freedom Blvd. (p.99)

Harkins Slough Rd.

This is a lightly travelled, narrow road just west of downtown Watsonville. It travels past a jail, cow pastures, orchards, a school and a few homes, and is one of the more enjoyable roads in the immediate area.

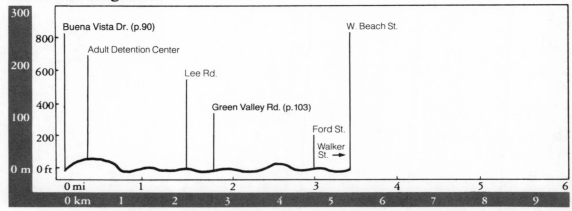

Buena Vista Dr. (p.90)
Adult Detention Center
Lee Rd.
Green Valley Rd. (p.103)
W. Beach St.
Ford St.
Walker St. →

Highway 1

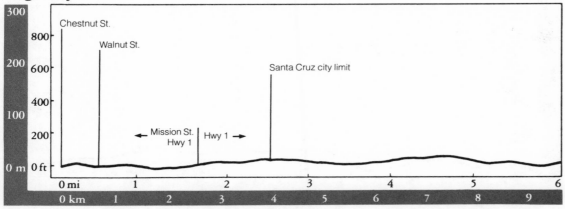

The coast highway in Santa Cruz Co. provides some interesting riding, but probably the major reason for its popularity is that it travels a flat and direct route between coastal settlements and farmland. It has a good surface with a decent shoulder, and cars, trailers, and motor homes move by fast and frequently. There are a couple of worthwhile diversions off this road—Swanton Rd., which loops back to the Highway, and Bonny Doon Rd., which leads to

Highway 1 *cont.*

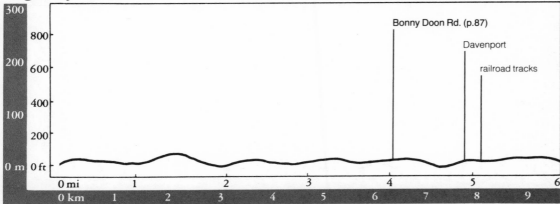

Empire Grade and eventually to Santa Cruz. Both of these alternatives are more time consuming and present more hills, but they also have less wind and carry less traffic.

Highway 1 *cont.*

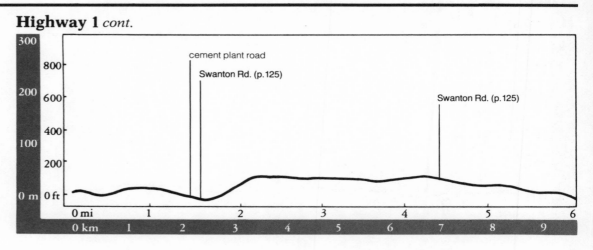

cement plant road

Swanton Rd. (p.125)

Swanton Rd. (p.125)

Highway 1 *cont.*

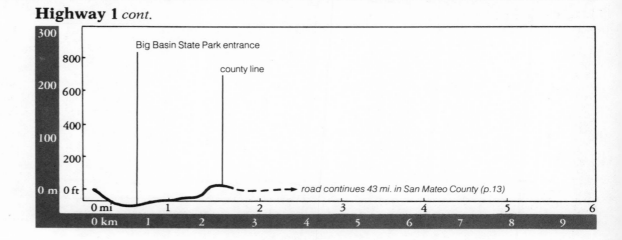

Big Basin State Park entrance

county line

road continues 43 mi. in San Mateo County (p.13)

Highway 9

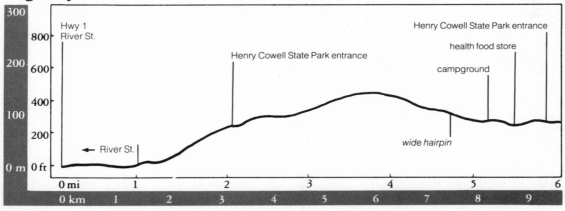

This road carries a lot of traffic, especially between Santa Cruz and Boulder Creek. Although there are bike lanes and the roadside attractions are pretty enough (redwoods, creeks), the traffic foils your ability to fully enjoy them. If you've got the time and the legs for it, pick an alternative, hillier route, such as Empire Grade. North of Boulder Creek the road is wider, and while the traffic moves faster here, it is somewhat less bothersome. By far

Highway 9 *cont.*

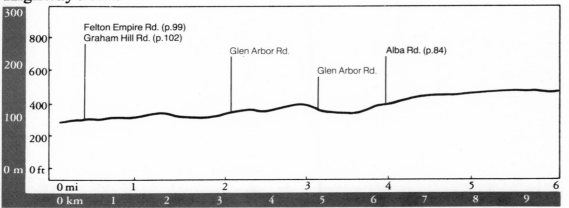

the most enjoyable aspect of riding this part of Highway 9 is the descent from Skyline Blvd.—the turns are gentle and well-banked, and allow a rider to approach the speed of the traffic. The higher elevations of this road are often embedded in a thick layer of fog, so if you ride early or late in the day, bright clothing will be particularly valuable.

Highway 9 *cont.*

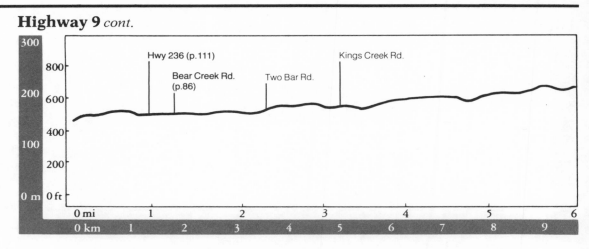

Highway 9 *cont.*

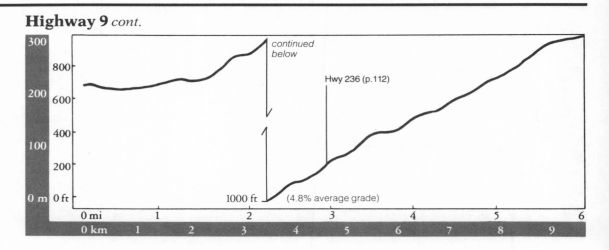

Highway 9 *cont.*

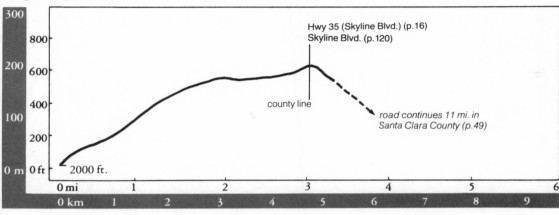

Hwy 35 (Skyline Blvd.) (p.16)
Skyline Blvd. (p.120)

county line

road continues 11 mi. in
Santa Clara County (p.49)

2000 ft.

Highway 17 Frontage Roads

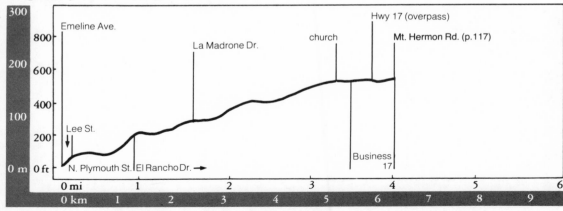

Emeline Ave.

La Madrone Dr.

church

Hwy 17 (overpass)

Mt. Hermon Rd. (p.117)

Lee St.

N. Plymouth St. El Rancho Dr. →

Business
17

This group of roads parallels Hwy 17 on the east side between Santa Cruz and Scotts Valley. The southern end is located near the junction of Hwy 17 and Hwy 1, beginning at Emeline Ave. as Lee St., which quickly becomes N. Plymouth St. The route passes through land that is somewhat developed, but portions of it are shaded and really pretty. The surface is well maintained and the traffic, while not light, is bearable.

This Santa Cruz County section of Hwy 152 has a smooth surface with an ample shoulder, and climbs up relatively undeveloped hillsides to the southern border of Mt. Madonna County Park. Unfortunately, it carries too much traffic to be a really enjoyable cycling road.

Highway 152 (East Lake Ave. / Hecker Pass Rd.)

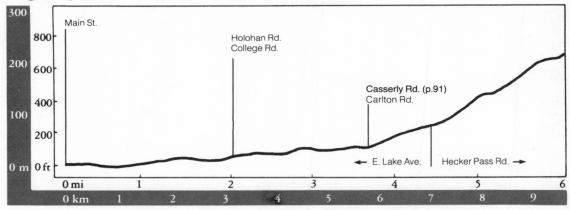

Highway 152 (East Lake Ave. / Hecker Pass Rd.) *cont.*

Highway 236

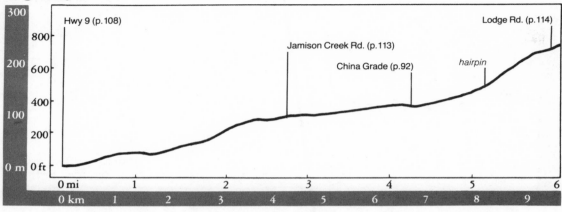

Hwy 9 (p.108)

Jamison Creek Rd. (p.113)

China Grade (p.92)

hairpin

Lodge Rd. (p.114)

This is a terrific road for bicyclists, even though it's a highway. It is very narrow, and takes you through Big Basin Redwoods State Park. Even those riders who aren't accustomed to stopping for a look at the landscape will do so here. Many of the turns are properly banked, and can be ridden through safely at a good speed. Although this road is also used by logging trucks, there are never very many—just be aware of them, especially on the

Highway 236 *cont.*

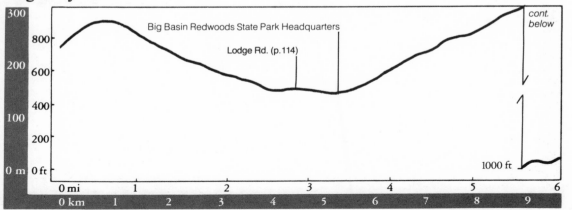

Big Basin Redwoods State Park Headquarters

Lodge Rd. (p.114)

cont. below

1000 ft

very narrow northern section. The Park Headquarters is a good place to stop, learn about the park, and re-fuel.

Highway 236 *cont.*

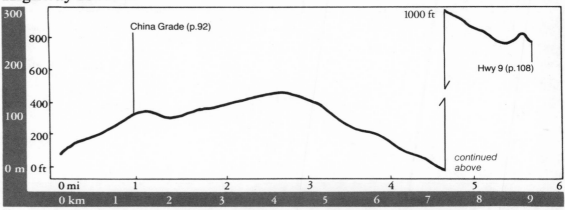

Ice Cream Grade

A narrow, very lightly travelled road that dips, climbs, and snakes through a forest of redwoods, madrones and oaks. It is located north of the town of Bonny Doon, high up in the Santa Cruz Mountains between Pine Flat Rd. and Empire Grade. The eastern end of it is somewhat residential.

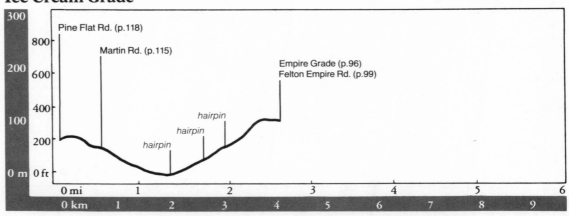

Swanton Rd.

Eureka Canyon Rd.

Jamison Creek Rd.

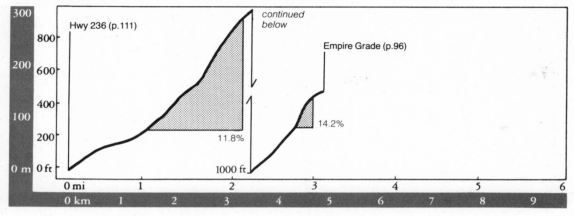

This road rivals Alba Rd. for being the most strenuous short climb in the Santa Cruz Mountains. It's a narrow road, and it winds up a forested hillside between Hwy 236 and Empire Grade. No road this steep is great fun to descend, because you find yourself more concerned about controlling your speed and making the turns than you are with the joys of fast, effortless riding. The traffic is light, but increases noticeably during commute hours.

Larkin Valley Rd.

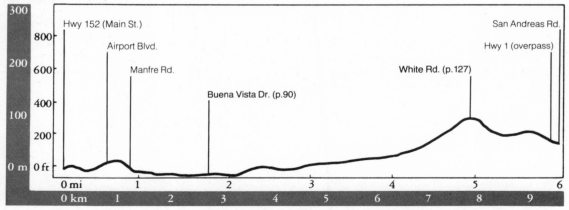

The southeastern tip of this road is residential, but the houses soon give way to a more rural setting in a quiet farm valley, with pastureland and stands of oak and eucalyptus. The hilly, northernmost couple of miles are the most scenic and enjoyable. Traffic is light.

Laurel Glen Rd. / Mountain View Rd.

These roads connect the north end of Branciforte Drive and Soquel-San Jose Road. They are narrow, wooded, and rural with a moderately rough surface and light local traffic.

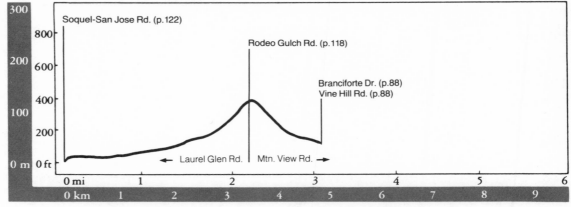

Lodge Rd.

This is a narrow, very pretty, and very lightly travelled road in Big Basin Redwoods State Park. Both ends connect to Hwy 236, and it winds through the shade of redwoods, oaks, and occasional madrones. It travels alongside a small canyon and a tiny creek, and passes an un-expectedly large waterfall which is easy to miss through the dense foliage. This is the type of road that you'll wish would go on for miles and miles.

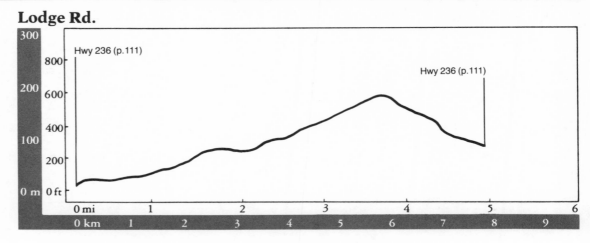

Loma Prieta Ave.

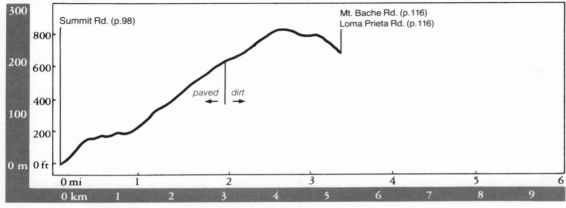

An enjoyable and very lightly travelled road on the ridge dividing Santa Cruz and Santa Clara Counties. It begins as a rough rural road, and quickly turns parallel to Highland Way, rising above it in a series of tiers past pear orchards and groves of Christmas trees. The dirt section snakes along a steep hillside covered with coyote bush, oak, and pine. You get a fantastic view of the valley below, and the feeling of being far away from civilization.

Martin Rd.

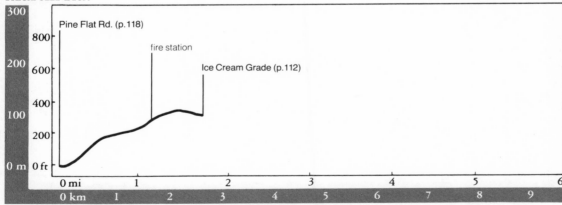

This road is a lot like neighboring Ice Cream Grade and Pine Flat Rd., high up in the Santa Cruz Mountains west of Henry Cowell Redwoods State Park. It's narrow, somewhat residential, has an abrasive, though not particularly bumpy surface, and travels through stands of conifers and eucalyptus. Very light traffic, a nice road.

Mountain Charlie Rd.

This road was named after Mountain Charlie McKiernan, whose story you can read on a plaque erected alongside the road. It travels through a beautiful mixed forest; the traffic is very light and the riding is great. It's well shaded, so don't wear sunglasses on the rather bumpy descent regardless of the weather, as your eyes will have a hard time making the necessary quick adjustments. The intersection with Summit Rd. is unmarked, and easy to miss.

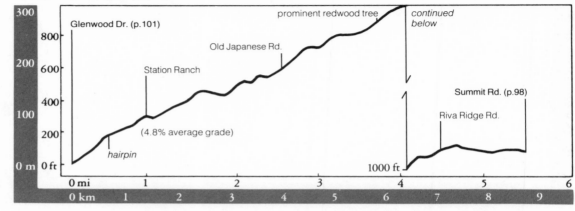

Mount Bache Rd. / Loma Prieta Rd.

Mt. Bache Road is a paved, but very rough residential road. It becomes Loma Prieta Rd. at the junction of Loma Prieta Ave. Continuing upwards, it becomes less developed as the surface turns to dirt and rock. The final push to the top is as rough a road as 1¼" tires can handle, and anything fatter will be appreciated. The end of the road provides you with a great view of the surrounding land. There is little shade, little traffic, and excellent, challenging riding.

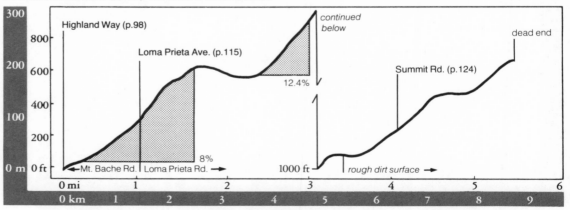

Mount Hermon Rd.

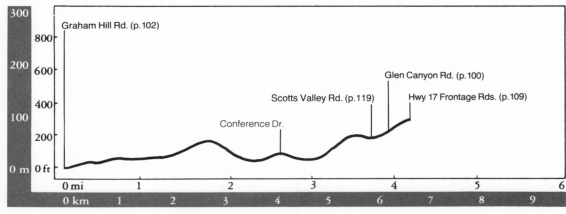

This is a major artery between Felton and Scotts Valley, so naturally, it's not a particularly pleasurable road for bicyclists. Fortunately, it has bike lanes, and it's useful.

Mount Madonna Rd.

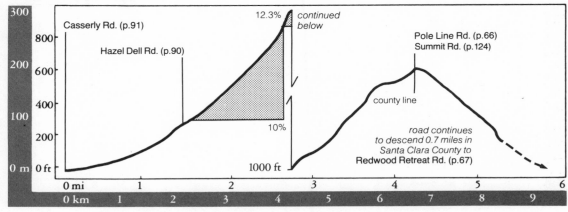

The initial mile and a half of this road is quiet and rural. At the Hazel Dell Rd. junction, it begins a grueling open climb above Browns Valley on a narrow surface. The upper part winds more and is shaded by redwoods. From its summit it descends through a dense and particularly beautiful redwood forest, on a graded gravel surface. The western part can be quite busy on summer weekends, but at other times the traffic is moderate to light.

Pine Flat Rd.

No matter which direction you approach this road from, you've got to do a lot of climbing. Its lower, southern end is located west of Henry Cowell State Park and north of the town of Bonny Doon, up in the Santa Cruz Mountains. It has a dark, smooth surface and climbs through stands of pine, oak, laurel, redwood and occasional eucalyptus trees. The traffic is generally very light, and the riding is enjoyable.

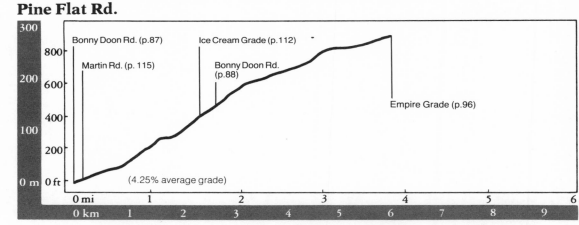

Rodeo Gulch Rd.

This begins as a smooth-surfaced residential road. As it climbs, it takes you through a forest of oaks and madrones, eventually meeting Mountain View Rd. The upper part is less travelled, unshaded, narrow, unkempt, and provides a good view of the valley below. It's a nice road.

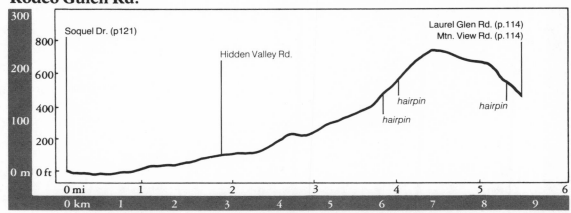

Scotts Valley Rd.

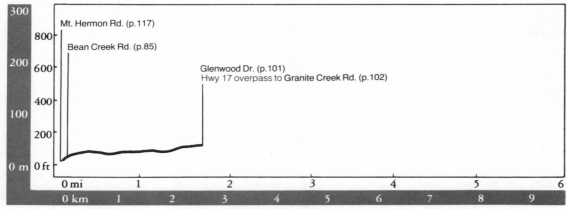

This is a busy, urban road that passes through the town of Scotts Valley. It won't provide you with any wonderful memories, but it will take you to better riding on Glenwood Dr. and Granite Creek Rd. There are bike lanes.

Skyland Rd.

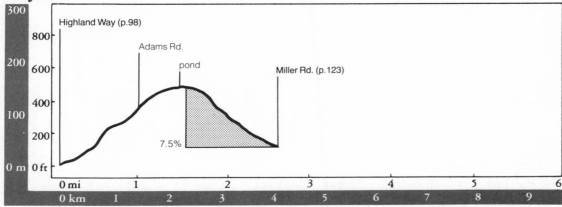

A narrow, winding, slightly residential road between Highland Way and Miller Rd. It travels through redwoods, madrones, and poison oak, past a few orchards along the way. A very pretty road, with light local traffic.

Skyline Blvd.

This road, like all Skylines, travels along, up and down the high flanks of a long ridge—in this case that of the Santa Cruz Mountains. From Bear Creek Rd. to Black Rd. it is shaded by oaks and buckeyes, and looks very much like Summit Rd. just south of Bear Creek Rd. The road here is a 1¼ lane wisp where you probably won't see a single car, and it should be ridden with particular care, as the occasional motorist won't be expecting to see a bicyclist either.

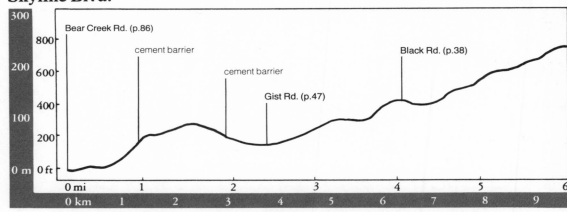

Skyline Blvd. *cont.*

From Black Rd. to Hwy 9 the traffic increases slightly, becoming fairly steady north of Hwy 9 and on into San Mateo County.

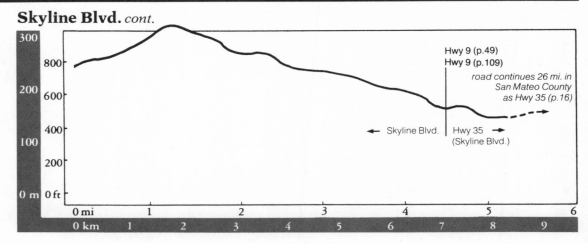

Smith Grade

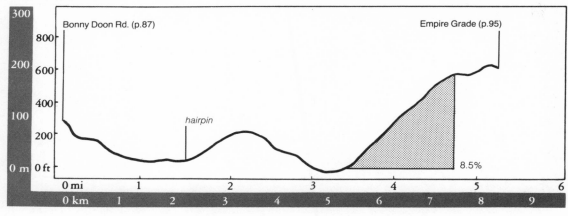

This is another beautiful road high up in the network of roads west of Henry Cowell Redwoods State Park. It's less travelled than the others though, and the road surface is generally rougher and littered with forest debris. It traverses the forested hills between Bonny Doon Rd. and Empire Grade, and if you like Martin, Pine Flat, Ice Cream Grade, and upper Bonny Doon Rd., you'll like this one, too.

Soquel Dr.

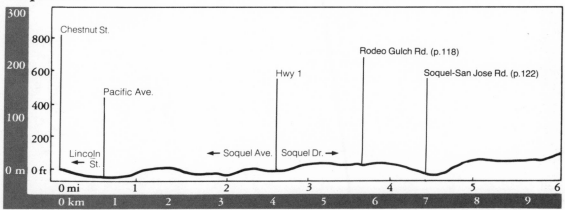

For those who drive, this is the alternative to the freeway between Santa Cruz and Aptos. It's a fairly direct route between the two towns, passing through business districts, and has a lot of traffic. It has no aesthetic appeal for bicyclists, but does have bike lanes, and can be useful.

Soquel Dr. *cont.*

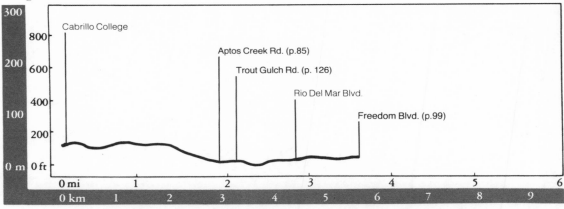

Soquel-San Jose Rd.

In many ways, this road is a scaled-down version of Bear Creek Rd. with the same dark, smooth surface, good shoulder, slightly to moderately bothersome traffic, and many gentle turns. It travels through the forested and somewhat residential hills between the town of Soquel and Highland Way. Despite the name, it doesn't get very close to San Jose.

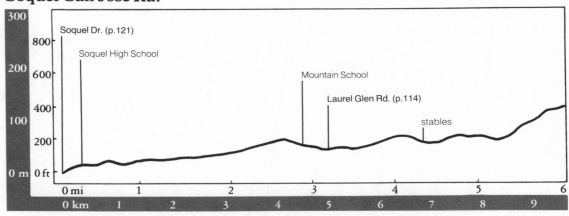

Soquel-San Jose Rd. *cont.*

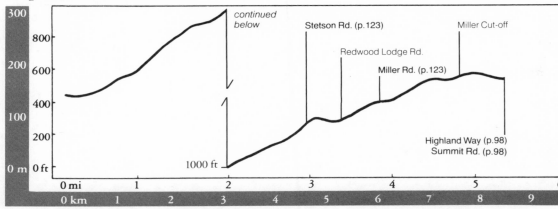

Stetson Rd. / Miller Rd.

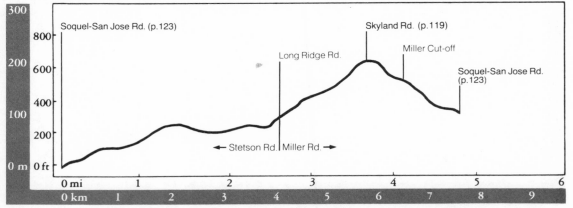

These are a pair of beautiful residential roads near Highland Way, off Soquel-San Jose Road. They're very narrow, winding, and shaded, traveling past lush hillsides. You'll feel like riding slowly and enjoying yourself, rather than trying to make time. The traffic is very light and local; a greater hazard is presented by the turns, which are narrow and sharp enough to require your full attention.

The lower three miles or so of this road are paved and travel over quiet, shady residential hillsides. The rest of the road is all dirt, and rolls along the upper part of a mountain ridge separating Santa Cruz and Santa Clara Counties. It's a beautiful, thoroughly enjoyable ride if you take it south from Loma Prieta Rd.; riding it the other direction, while just as beautiful, is a heck of a lot more strenuous. In either case, you'll get excellent views of the dis-

Summit Rd.

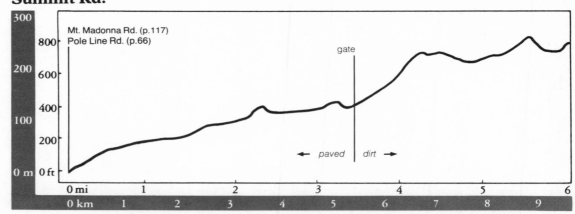

tant mountains and valleys. Although it's a dirt road, narrow wheels will work just fine if ridden with a little care, but if you have a ballooner you might as well ride it here. The land around this road belongs to a coalition of homeowners called the Summit Road Association. They've put up gates with signs that say something to the effect of KEEP OUT, but the road itself is public—just keep off the private land around it.

Summit Rd. *cont.*

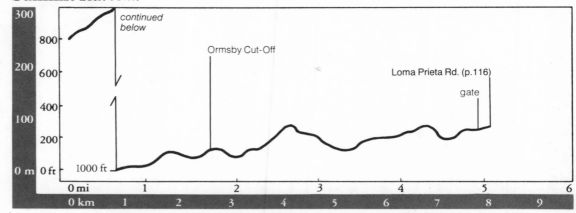

Swanton Rd.

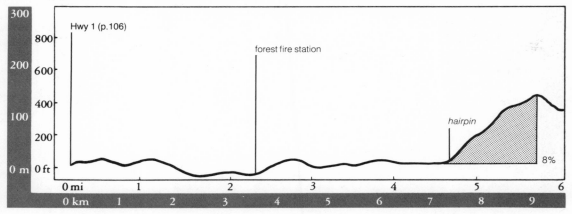

This is a great diversion off Hwy 1, about 10 miles north of Santa Cruz. The southern portion takes you over rolling farmland, past a few residences and a fire station. The northern half of it is even less developed and travels over hills above a canyon, through a forest of buckeyes, oaks, redwoods, and aspens. Heading south on Hwy 1, the northern end of it is easy to miss—look for it about a mile south of Waddell Beach. Light traffic.

Swanton Rd. *cont.*

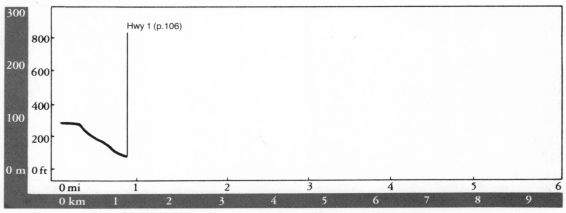

Trout Gulch Rd.

This road begins as a smooth-surfaced rural road, curving gently past scattered orchards and residences. After a couple of miles it narrows, the surface gets rougher, and it winds through the shade of redwood, oak, and maple trees growing on hillsides covered with ferns and assorted bushes. It ends at Fern Flat Rd., near the south-eastern border of The Forest of Nisene Marks State Park. Light traffic.

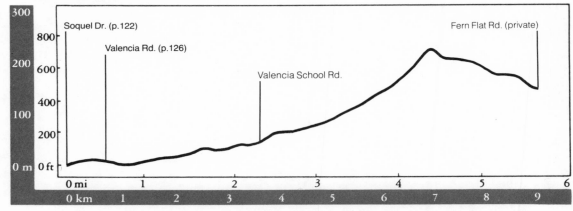

Valencia Rd.

Valencia is a narrow, rather pretty road in a network of simi-lar roads northeast of Aptos. It passes redwoods, follows along-side Valencia Creek, then cros-ses the creek to a forested hill-side. Light traffic, and enjoyable.

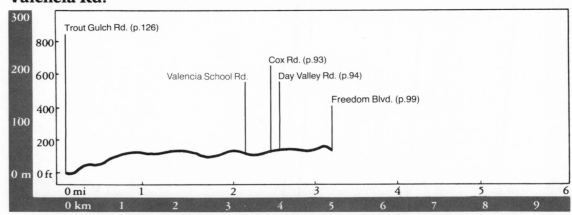

Varni Rd. / Pioneers Rd.

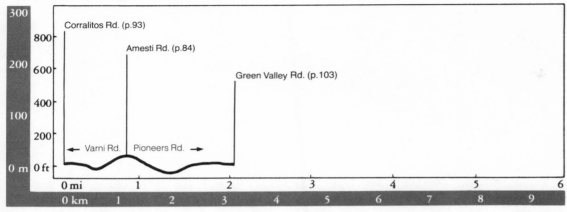

These two roads connect Corralitos Rd. and Green Valley Rd. They're narrow, have a small gravel shoulder, light local traffic, and travel past orchards and farm houses.

White Rd.

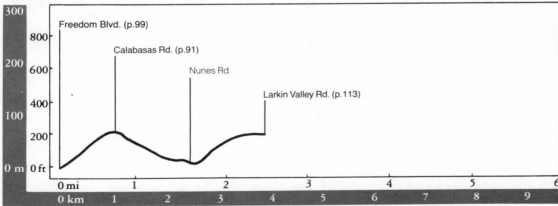

A short, narrow, rural road northwest of Watsonville. It's a pretty road, and passes through stands of eucalyptus and oak trees on hillsides splattered with ferns and poison oak. Only light, local traffic.

Page Mill Rd.

BART

You can take your bike on BART just once without a *BART Bicycle Permit*. If you want a permit, write for an application. The address is:

BART Bicycle Permit
800 Madison Street
Oakland, CA 94607

or phone (415) 465-4100, x569

The cost is $3.00 and the permit is good for 3 years. When you get your permit you'll also receive sheet of rules and bicycle-legal hours.

Bridges

Hayward-San Mateo Bridge:
No riding allowed. You can be shuttled across on a Caltrans maintenance vehicle providing it isn't needed for official use, but you must make arrangements 24 hours in advance. Phone Caltrans at (415) 464-0876 or 464-0699 for more information.

Dumbarton Bridge:
Riding allowed in the bike lane.

About the Authors

Grant Petersen was born in the Bay Area in 1954, and has lived here all his life. He began riding bicycles extensively in 1973, and rides roughly 250 days a year. He has toured several thousand miles and races competitively, but prefers brisk day rides in the Bay Area hills. He enjoys a variety of outdoor pursuits, photography, and cooking. He currently works in the bicycle industry.

John Kluge was born in the San Francisco Bay Area in 1959, and has resided here ever since. He began to run seriously at age 11, and began to cycle in 1981. Preferring hilly terrain to city traffic, he frequents the hills around Berkeley and Oakland. Since 1981, he has worked in an outdoor sporting goods store in Berkeley.

Index